Going Deep

Reflections on Challenge and Change

Pam Gardiner

Copyright © 2014 by Pam Gardiner

All rights reserved. This book or any portion thereof may not be reproduced or used in any manner whatsoever without the express written permission of the publisher except for the use of brief quotations in a book review. Printed in the United States of America

First Printing, 2014

ISBN-13:978-1500164041

Pam Gardiner
www.wellbuddies.com

for Jane

We bookend the Baby Boom: I was born in 1946, she in 1963. The daily correspondence of our early friendship grew into a weekly email, *Reflections*, sent to a wider audience. It all started with Jane. In 2013 she and the other youngest Baby Boomers turned 50. Happy Birthday, and thank you so very much.

Contents

Preface

Balance 1

Flamingo or Bicycle? 2

Small Not-doings 3

Rubber Hits the Road 4

Who Am I Now? 5

More Time for What? 6

Inside-Out 7

Choices in Heaven and Hell 8

Holding Close and Letting Go 9

Calming the Chatter 10

Plant, Water, Watch 11

Laws of Motion 12

Dancing with Yin and Yang 13

Mary Gets a Bye 14

Adventure 15

It's About the Journey 16

Speaking and Dancing 17

A Hundred Miles of Opportunity 18

Triumph in the Alps 19

Flying off the Cliff 20

I Can Do It! 21

Rear-view Mirror 22

The Writer's Nest 23

Caution on the Edge 24

The Book Project 25

Together on the Field of Play 26

Now We Are Three 27

When Pigs Fly 28

Front and Back 29

Detour 31

Times of Midlife Change 32

Demons and Dead Ends 33

Asking for Directions 34

Six Weeks in a Sling 35

Sight-shifting 36

The Restart Button 37

More Questions than Answers 38

Choose Life 39

Missions, Malfunctions, and Miracles 40

I Feel Your Strength 41

A Time and a Season 42

Holy Days 43

Perspective 45

Serenity, Courage, and Wisdom 46

Future and Presence 47

In Exile or at Home? 48

Doors and Windows 49

Dream and Nightmare 50

How Full is Your Glass? 51

Thank You for Being a Pain 52

Ordinary Lives 53

Wedding and Funeral 54

To Celebrate or Not 55

Getting Into It 56

Living with Joy 57

Calling 59

Exactly Where We Need to Be 60

Lessons My Father Taught Me 61

Mother Taught Me, Too 62

Retirement: Surprise! 63

Looking Forward, Looking Back 64

Can't Stop Talking 65

Find Your Strong 66

Now You Can Stop 67

Faith in the Fog 68

Easter, Sixto, and the Four Seasons 69

Morning Prayers 70

When I Grow Up 71

Labyrinth in Life 72

Connection 73

Sparks and Smooth Edges 74

Gratitude Alert 75

Reconnecting with Love 76

Flu Season 77

Family Ties, Bows, and Knots 78

Peas and Butter, Mother and Me 79

Tree Casts a Shadow 80

How Can I Help? 81

Tripping Over Sweetie 82

Thinking of You 83

May I Take Control? 84

Weaving on the Web 85

Energy 87

Renewable Energy 88

Flow and the Fourth of July 89

Whitewater 90

White Space 91

Frame It and Paint It 92

Investing the Gift 93

Counting Sheep 94

Fight, Flee, Embrace 95

Bang! Bang! Pause 96

How Are You? 97

Hoarding and Sorting 98

Let There Be Light 99

People Power 100

Seasons 101

Winter Driving 102

Shades of Gray 103

April Showers 104

Dust Bunnies 105

Alaskan Summer 106

Longest Day 107

Dry Lightning 108

Cooler, Darker, Busier 109

Tipping the Balance 110

Fall Back, Play it Again 111

Grateful Anyway 112

Solstice 113

Afterword

Resources

Acknowledgments

Author

Preface

Born in 1963, the youngest Baby Boomers recently turned 50. With that passage, a new generation is plunging into the adventure of midlife change. We Boomers have been together for a long time. Born in a wave 77-million strong following World War II, we were raised by Dr. Spock and grew up filled with hope and expectation. As we matured we developed our own culture, a culture of questioning and challenging authority, inventing and re-inventing ourselves. As we approach the golden years, we are determined to do it our way.

We resist calling midlife a crisis. We don't let things get us down. Still, we confront the changes happening around us and within. Our children have moved out, and maybe our spouses. We are retiring, ready or not. Parents need us in new ways. Our bodies signal the need for attention. Midlife is a time of challenge and we are rising to that challenge in creative ways.

Born in 1946, I belong to the first wave of Boomers and have been exploring life-after-50 for some time now. I have enjoyed the process of reflecting in writing on the experiences I face, looking for different ways of looking at challenge and change. This book began as a personal journal, and then grew into email conversations with my best friend. Over time, it turned into a weekly email with an expanding network of fans and friends. When they asked if I would collect their favorite essays and publish a book, I said yes.

I wrote the essays in this book to deepen and share my perspective on the challenge of living. My reflections on everyday experience draw from many sources, including the spiritual journey and favorite inspirational authors. I also find value in scientific understanding of the brain and the dynamics of personal change. I play with words and enjoy the insights that arise from metaphor and myth. And I draw lessons from the stories of others: heroes, role models, and friends.

I hope this book helps you deepen your own engagement with living. We all face tough times; we get discouraged and are tempted to give up. We are also gifted with profound sources of resilience that enable us to alter our approach, modify our thinking, fire up our creativity, and make the best of any new experience when it comes along.

This is not a how-to book; it does not offer tips and tricks for managing midlife change. It is, rather, an invitation to develop your own strategies for rising to the challenge. Each essay is built around personal experience. It explores that experience from various angles and ends with questions that toss the ball to you: How does this experience resonate in your own life? How might you approach the challenge more creatively the next time it comes around?

Balance

*Happiness is not a matter of intensity
but of balance and order and rhythm and harmony.*
Thomas Merton

As we grow, the explosion of opportunity challenges us to achieve a life of dynamic and harmonic balance. From day to day and hour to hour, we adjust the allocation of time and energy between contrasting extremes: productivity and play, structure and serendipity, solitude and sociability. This first chapter of our shared adventure offers a glimpse of life balance in its many forms. Later chapters will revisit the subject as viewed through a rich variety of experience, perspective, and choice.

Flamingo or Bicycle?

The subject of life balance comes up in many of my conversations, and I'll bet it comes up in yours. Our work. Our families. Our friendships. Our fitness. Our passions. Our obligations. They don't all fit at the same time, yet they are all important. Overload!

Let's consider "the tree," an especially challenging pose for beginning yoga students. In tree pose, we are asked to stand on one foot, the other foot perched on the inner thigh, hands reaching skyward like a flamingo dancing a ballet. When I think of balance in terms of yoga and flamingoes, the possibility escapes me. How long can I maintain balance on one foot, even if I do gaze at a fixed point on the wall? And how can I afford to focus on one point when I must attend to dozens more?

Enter the bicycle. Now we are getting somewhere! A bicycle also calls for balance, but it is different; it is balance-in-motion. The bicycle balances, not on a point but along a trajectory. It calls for constant adjustment to changes in the road, in the wind, in the flow of traffic. A bicycle can be loaded with cargo when necessary or stripped down if speed is important. I can relate to the bicycle better than the flamingo as a symbol of balance in my life.

Balance is not achieved at a moment in time; it unfurls gradually. It cannot be captured in a day, but accumulates step by step over weeks and months. When I flip through the calendar at year's end, what balance of priorities do I see? Some weeks were all about the job. Some were about family or friends. Some were devoted to taxes, plumbing, or a balky computer. Perhaps I even took a few days for retreat and reflection.

I monitor my personal life-balance meter by the month. Where am I overdoing? What am I neglecting? Do I want to add or phase things out in the weeks ahead? When I pay periodic attention to questions like these, I am more likely to celebrate a rich, well-rounded year in review than to regret the opportunities left behind.

__Imagine riding a bicycle through the month ahead. Where are you going? What hazards lie along the way? How will you maintain momentum and remain upright in the process?__

Small Not-doings

Cheryl gave me the book for Christmas: *Simple Living*, a slim volume written by José Hobday, an American Indian nun. Sister José draws both from Native culture and life in a religious community to show that simplicity makes room in our lives for whatever is truly important. She writes about streamlining our food, clothing, transportation, housing, work, and recreation. I find that the effort to simplify is a valuable tool in the quest for life balance. The fewer dishes I pile in one stack, the more easily I can carry them to the kitchen; the fewer choices I entertain at once, the more easily I can fit them harmoniously into the available time.

The attraction of living more simply grows as I age. With the years, I have accumulated not only more "stuff" but also a growing list of interests, passions, and promises made; more friends; more activities, organizations, and causes; a longer list of things to see and do. One computer gave rise to two because I wanted to hang out in coffee shops to write on a laptop. A love of reading has only grown with the magic of e-books and the one-click online purchase. My new gym has more machines, a bigger pool, and a track. With three flavors of cold cereal, I always have a choice. And how many pairs of black shoes do I need?

I hear underlying questions about life balance, both from Sister José and from my own inner voice. Do more options lead to greater happiness? Would my life be more joyful if I ate the same combination of oatmeal and fruit every morning or if I wore the same outfit to work at home three days in a row?

When considering New Year's goals, a friend lamented, "I just can't add one more thing." Another friend wrote: "My challenge is to not-do some small things and create space for bigger things." I have seized the phrase "small not-doings" and made it my own. How about a not-to-do list? We add and less often remove: unread magazines, classes we want to take, home improvement projects, social events, or technological wonders.

Where can you create space in your life to balance doing with deliberate not-doing? What higher priority might fill that gap?

Rubber Hits the Road

We had a big snowstorm the week before Christmas. It seemed that the trusty Subaru was slipping more than usual, no longer plowing its way through winter like a reliable tank. Facing a holiday highway trip, I stopped by the tire shop.

Legally bald! How could that be? When were the tires last balanced and wheels aligned? Oops! Without proper alignment and balance, rubber hits the road unevenly. Tires no longer aim in the same direction. They wobble and wear and lose their grip.

Buying new tires was a startling and costly lesson, especially during the holiday season. The experience also provided valuable material for reflection. I discovered that it is important not only to re-balance and align our cars on a regular schedule, but also to re-balance, align, and watch for signs of wear in our lives.

A few weeks later, I was slipping and sliding again. This time, it was not about tires. It was about commitments. When I volunteered to coach a marathon training program, I misjudged the time and effort it would require. I did not recognize the need to modify earlier promises in making space for the new one. Before long, I was unbalanced and misaligned, wearing down and slipping on curves.

Eventually I adjusted and again rolled straight, tracking with the road. The impulsive decision to take on a new task had thrown me off balance at first. But the joys of volunteering for rewarding work won out, and I set other commitments aside without regret. The wheels were all pointed in the same direction and the tires were balanced for the trip ahead.

How does this story apply to you? Are you slipping and sliding more than usual? Pause, step back, balance, and align. Get a grip.

Who Am I Now?

I have long idealized the simplicity of monastic life: a single bed, desk, and chair; a uniform clothing style; a prescribed schedule. It seems in my romantic view as if many sources of pain and difficulty would vanish if I had less clutter in my life. As a result, I go through recurring cycles of purging, attacking the piles and looking for ways to carve out more space around the things I keep.

Each time I do so, I hit the same wall between a desire to streamline and attachment to the things I try to unload. During a recent encounter, I reflected on the dynamics of sentimental value, exploring the emotional overtones of cards and letters, photographs, awards, and other reminders of past times.

I found that my sense of self clings tightly to reminders. It goes through the drawers and boxes, checking off races run, books read, degrees earned, and mountains climbed. I describe myself and evaluate my worth in those terms, and at some level I fear that I will forget and perhaps even lose something intrinsically "me" if I clean out the closet and give things away.

When I feel clear and content, however, I welcome the view that only the present moment is real. The events and experiences of the past are not. They divert my attention from the present and tempt me to get lost in what-once-was. It's hard to release a reminder of past joy, but I feel a little lighter after doing so.

As we age, the collections of the years expand, becoming bulky and heavy. They fill our space, our minds, and our hearts. The monastic ideal retreats into the ever-more impossible distance. Or maybe not. I still aspire to living with a lighter touch. I want to reduce cravings and release attachments. I am looking for the right balance between past and future so that I can take my hand off the controls and enjoy the moment.

What is your relationship with mementoes? How can you honor the experiences that made you who you are today, without clinging too tightly to the past?

More Time for What?

The dimensions of life balance include time, effort, energy, and attention. When I feel overwhelmed, it feels like a shortage of time. For that reason, I love white space on the calendar and embrace the value of limiting commitments. I typically invest that "free" time in recharging batteries for the active life. I read, take a solitary run, or indulge in an extended nap with the cat. A recent conversation, however, suggested additional ways in which ample time could improve the quality of living.

My response to others, especially to those who appear without an "appointment," is often aggravated when I feel overscheduled. I am annoyed by the telemarketer on the phone or a stranger at the door. I postpone visiting a lonely neighbor and fidget impatiently when my partner expounds on a topic that bores me. Perhaps a less crowded schedule would make room for unplanned exchanges like these, as well as providing for recovery from busier times.

I find it humbling to reflect on the dismissive tone I reserve for unknown callers and my reluctance to answer the doorbell, much less interact respectfully with the person on the other side. How much time does it take to treat strangers with kindness? Not much. How much effort does it take to overcome resentment about the interruption? A lot. I interpret an unexpected call or doorbell as an affront, as I always have something that feels more important to do.

All spiritual traditions counsel kindness. They urge us to respect and care for those in need, those who are poor, weak, and ill. We may not see the person at the door or on the phone in that light, but what if we did? They are making a living. They are raising funds for a cause that is important to them. They are sharing the good news of their religious faith. Does my religious faith teach me to slam down the phone or ignore the doorbell when it rings? Not really. I want to practice dealing with them differently and see where it takes me.

How do you deal with interruptions? Do you resent those who intrude, or do you respond with generous sensitivity? Might you try something different the next time?

Inside-Out

Midlife is a wonderful time to find new sources of purpose and meaning in our lives. In our youth, we looked for success in concrete achievement. We worked for good grades, social popularity, and athletic performance in school. We pursued income, benefits, promotion, and recognition at work. We wanted the health and happiness of partners, children, siblings, and parents in our families. We set standards of success for our roles as volunteers, learners, leaders, and activists.

Then one day, we find the questions about success going deeper, sometimes with surprising results. What does it mean to be happy? It may have more to do with acceptance than control. Unconditional love brings more peace than forcing others to meet our needs. Stopping to savor a colorful sunset rewards us more than checking one more project off the list. Listening open-heartedly to a loved one feels better than challenging their views and asserting our own.

I have spent a lifetime viewing myself in terms of success and failure in school, with people, in sport, and at work. I am good at philosophy, terrible at statistics. A good friend but not-so-great a hostess. Adequate runner, abysmal skier. An effective planner who struggles with the details of getting things done. The list of strengths and deficits has lengthened with the years. In midlife, I want to shed that list and raise my sense of self and life purpose to a higher level. I live. I love. I enjoy. I accept. I appreciate. I am present.

It is never all one way or the other; pursuing life with purpose and meaning calls for balance. Practical demands and the projects we take on will always call for effort and provide us with concrete rewards. In balance, however, a deeper spirit emanates from within and grows with age.

What does your spirit have to say about the higher and broader purpose in your life? What aspects of success are fading in importance with time?

Choices in Heaven and Hell

"Heaven is having a choice; hell is having to choose." Morris Massey introduced me to that phrase more than 30 years ago in a talk about generational differences. He pointed out that we Boomers had created the salad bar, and that was a big deal at the time. Any trip through a grocery store, electronics outlet, or website today shows the extremes to which we have gone in generating a heaven of options. I am still confounded by the hell of choosing only one. That hell can reach a new level of intensity when we retire.

I often reflect on the gift of free time—the opportunity to choose what to do and when. In retirement, we may also be faced with choosing what to do, period. So many books, so little time. So many causes and needy people. So many trips. So many fitness goals. So many projects around the house and yard. The options are never exhausted, though the process of exploring them all may drive us to exhaustion.

Other retirees seem to accomplish so much more than I do. They travel constantly. They build new homes, remodel, and landscape. They care for their own young children, grandchildren, or elders; serve on boards; set up businesses; or all of those plus more. How do they do it?

It has taken me a while to let go of that question. It misses the point. Their choices have nothing to do with mine. This is a time in life for outgrowing the urge to compare and for pursuing the values that mean the most to each of us. One of my deepest retirement values is to maintain a slower pace than I did while working.

What is so great about slow? Doesn't it just mean I am getting less of the retirement pie than those who manage a faster pace? I don't see it that way anymore. With continual adjustment, I am honing a pace that serves as its own reward. It seeks out mental and social stimulation, to a point. It is active, within limits. It volunteers and works and produces and serves, then stops to reflect. The magic pace for me is fast enough to stay awake, but slow enough to breathe. Runners call it a "conversational pace." I want the beauty and wisdom I encounter to sink in, not whiz by.

As I balance my choices between reading and parties, gallery walks and evenings at home, taking a class and taking a nap, I am developing a rhythm of my own. I limit the hell of having to choose by scheduling a few events and goals, then letting life gently color in the white space on an empty calendar.

What is your ideal balance between hectic and leisurely? Do you fill the calendar to overflowing, or do you allow time for a detour, a friendly chat, or stopping to take pictures along the way?

Holding Close and Letting Go

May 15 was circled in red on the family calendar. Jonathan and Jennie had chosen that day for their wedding. As we prepared for this new stage of our parental journey, conflicting emotions bubbled to the surface. Those emotions were familiar, but still uncomfortable. Each new adventure took our son a little farther away.

As humans we are designed for attachment, yet we also have the powerful opposing urge to stand on our own. The emotional balance between connection and autonomy is a dynamic we face in friendship, on teams, and in families. How much do I ask that you change to please me, and how much do I change to accommodate you? What are acceptable thresholds between dependence, independence, and interdependence? How does one achieve intimacy while retaining identity?

Parenting presents a unique challenge to that emotional balance. Our babies start out as part of us, and then spend the rest of their lives becoming separate. Our role is to nurture and protect while enabling growth. There is no single balance point; the scales are always in motion.

There are, however, milestones: First day of kindergarten. First sleep-over. First date. Driver's license. College. Study abroad. Graduation. And now, in our family, marriage.

Their relationship had been incubating, and the shift had been taking place over time. We celebrated seeing our only child find lasting love. We looked forward to enlarging our own family picture to include Jennie and her family. On the other hand, the unique bond of emotional attachment that began with conception would be stretched by this decisive occasion. It would stretch us to embrace a new daughter and to let go as Jonathan and Jennie became a family of their own.

These changes are good ones, and they call for applause. They are also hard ones, and tears rise as we adjust to the new emotional balance.

What midlife transitions most challenge your emotions? How has the balance between holding close and letting go shifted in new and important ways?

Calming the Chatter

Those early humans who remained alert, watching and listening for predators, survived. Those who slept soundly or attended to one task at a time were eaten. That primitive bias is an advantage if we are driving on the freeway, constantly aware of what is happening and what could go wrong. It is a liability if we want to write an article, listen to a friend, or sleep soundly through the night.

I picked up this useful tidbit in reading *Buddha's Brain*. Neuroscientists Rick Hanson and Richard Mendius identify sensitive tuning and instinctive reactivity as primitive traits of the reptilian brain. The contrasting ability to focus by screening out distractions comes with the human prefrontal cortex. I am always looking for ways to improve the balance between outer awareness and inner concentration.

In the quest for better focus, I recently dropped a different distraction each day for a week: television, radio, newspaper, telephone, and online networking. On the final day I abstained from both email and Facebook, and thought I was going to die! I saw how much I lean on social networks to fill gaps in my schedule and to offer a shot of love when I feel lonely or sad.

The experiment was difficult, but it was also liberating. It created space in the day and unfamiliar pauses in the flow of mental chatter. It interrupted the immediacy between stimulus and response, relaxing the call to action.

Having fasted from online communication for a day, I am considering new restraints on my regular habits. Could I check email every few hours (not minutes)? Would Facebook taste better as a bedtime treat, not an hourly snack? I have not made those changes, but I am intrigued. I enjoy virtual connectedness and I value the ease of communication it represents. I also know that constant re-checking feeds the distracted mind and impedes the focus that evades my best effort much of the time.

What balance of mental variety and focused attention works for you? Are you easily bored, or more easily distracted? What practices would take you in the right direction?

Plant, Water, Watch

A few years ago, I discovered Paula Huston's *Simplifying the Soul,* a book of Lenten practices designed to foster life balance. For six weeks under her tutelage I performed daily experiments in seeing and doing things differently. The effort to simplify began with space and moved on to money, body, mind, time, and relationships. When Lent ended on Easter, I was inspired to harvest the seeds of simplicity and to sow them more broadly in my life.

The first seed is, perhaps, most obvious: It is not simple to simplify. Our culture is wired for increasing complexity. A hundred options confound every choice. Complicating sheer numbers is the implied mandate to make the best choice. How do we determine the ideal internet service, running shoe, spiritual practice, or volunteer opportunity? I have found that the simpler way makes a thoughtful choice, then releases those unseized opportunities without regret. Some of my choices will turn out poorly, and that's OK.

The second seed is more subtle: Simplicity is not just another goal. We can make a complicated project out of streamlining. We can develop detailed rulebooks around eating, relating, spending, praying, and thinking. In the process we might just exchange one form of mental and spiritual clutter for a new one. I have come to see the journey differently. My life is simpler if I struggle less for control, ask my inner wisdom for guidance, and trust it to take the lead.

Finally, simplicity is not an end in itself. It is a means to the end of pursuing my deepest values. I protect free time not only for self-indulgence, but also to be more available for others. I curb spending for my own rainy day, but also to give more freely when opportunities arise. I modify my standards of hospitality not only to avoid work and reduce guilt. I also want to welcome guests more easily, without obsessing over a cobweb or a microwaved meal.

Easter comes in spring. It is a time of new life, hope, and growth. The exercises in simplicity that I adopted from Paula Huston offered a variety of seeds. I want to choose a few, water them, and watch them grow.

Which aspects of a simpler and better balanced life speak most personally to you? Where would you like to plant those seeds, and how will you nurture them as they grow?

Laws of Motion

We learned from Sir Isaac Newton long ago that bodies at rest stay at rest and bodies in motion remain in motion, unless they experience some outside force. The same can be said of minds, hearts, and spirits. The principle applies to the whole person.

As I live and write about living, this principle grows in relevance to everyday life. I find the balancing act between stillness and action a work forever in progress. I experience a continual play of give and take in the desire for stability and the search for novelty, the instinct to withdraw and the urge to reach out, the integrity of sticking to a known path and the enticement of striking out cross-country.

The energy and ambition needed for physical activity, social engagement, self-improvement, and an unlimited flow of projects eventually wear thin. At those times, an outside force like a bad cold might insist that I stop. When I am lucky, I see disaster coming and repair the system before it collapses. I clear the calendar, put away unfinished projects, and pare down the list of things that really need to be done. The body in motion needs to pause and reflect.

I also have times when motivation grinds to a halt and my personal engine stalls out. On those occasions, I look for emotional jumper cables that will add some juice and kick me back into action. I recently came back exhausted from three weeks on the road. Both mind and body both collapsed for more than a week, asserting their need to recover. Once I stopped, it was hard to get moving again. I did mindless chores and ran pointless errands, but purposeful effort eluded me.

Then one morning I sat down and chained myself to the laptop with a commitment to write. Writing did not start smoothly. Those brain cells that pull thoughts and words together were reluctant, but they responded to exercise, stumbling into motion again at last. The body at rest needed extra effort to sputter back into action.

How do you stop when you're moving too fast or get started again after a pause? Which of those is your bigger challenge right now?

Dancing with Yin and Yang

I recently engaged in a lively discussion with friends about the traits of introversion and extroversion. Some clearly saw themselves in either the "I" or "E" camp, while others waffled with, "It depends." Some had taken an online survey that identified them as amibiverts, whatever that means. With all the fuzziness, is the distinction between introversion and extroversion useful, or just confusing?

I am one who typically answers the survey questions, "It depends" whether I react as an extrovert or introvert when the time comes. It depends on the party, and who I know there, whether I leave early or stay until it ends. It depends on the project whether I want to gather a team for brainstorming over beer or to spend that time alone with a laptop and coffee.

It can be challenging to assert the need for solitude when others don't see a need. Since I lean toward introversion but have typically worked on teams, I regularly teeter between extremes. Over the years, I have developed the following strategies for balancing sociability with solitude, conversation with inner silence.

I write. Writing nurtures my need to think things through and offsets the discomfort of speaking on my feet or deciding on the fly. The more time I spend mulling things over, the better the action that results.

I schedule solitude. I get up early to read, write, and meditate before engaging with other people and the outside world.

I monitor the calendar. When I see a surge of social activity on the horizon, I take extra care to retain white space between commitments and to plan for recovery after the surge has passed.

I seek out other introverts. We enjoy on-on-one conversations that get into depth. Finding a soul-mate at a party enhances an event designed by and for extroverts.

The experience of living and functioning in an extroverted society is a dance between opposites like yin and yang. On the one hand, we are connected; on the other hand we are individuals. Each of us has a unique way of moving back and forth between those poles in a way that optimizes energy and productivity.

Where do you see yourself in this picture? What strategies have you developed to deal with your own need for others and desire to be alone some of the time?

Mary Gets a Bye

In one of my favorite Bible stories, Jesus visits the home of two sisters, Martha and Mary (Luke 10:38-42). Martha makes sure the house is clean and the food is cooked. She is annoyed when Mary hangs out with the guests, listening to Jesus instead of helping with the chores. When asked to chide Mary for leaving her sister with all the work, Jesus replies that Mary had chosen the better part.

This is a controversial passage. No one is comfortable with the image of a hardworking hostess sweating over the stove while her lazy little sibling gets off with praise. In my view, the story illustrates the perpetual life-balancing tension between doing and being, production and presence, tasks and relationships.

I am by temperament and habit aligned with Mary. My life skills and comfort zone lie on the other side of a great divide from domestic prowess. I am, therefore, relieved by Jesus' take on the situation. I would much rather listen to Him than prepare appetizers in the other room. It is tempting to feel justified and to leave it at that. On the other hand, my own life is often out of balance on this scale.

I want to spend more time with Martha, paying attention to practical concerns. If I don't change the oil, the engine will clog and seize. If I don't prepare healthy meals, fast food will add pounds before I know it. If I don't weed and prune, the vacuum nature is known to abhor will fill and overflow. I want to develop skills where there are gaps. I want to get on top of the basics.

On the other hand, Martha's work never ends and getting on top of household chores doesn't mean staying on top of them. I therefore accept the need to cut some corners and give Mary her turn. It is OK to meet friends at a café instead of inviting them for homemade. It is OK to revisit the frequency of laundry, dusting, and mopping. It is OK to ask whether Grandma's standards need apply to me now.

As I reflected on Martha and Mary this week, I found a poem on Facebook, *Dust if You Must* by Rose Milligan. It begins, "Dust if you must, but wouldn't it be better to paint a picture or write a letter?" Milligan's poem reinforced my desire to write about this stumbling block on the path to a balanced life. In honor of Martha, I spent an hour this morning weeding, and only then allowed Mary the time to write.

Are you more of a Mary or a Martha at heart? What small steps could you take to strengthen your other side? What do you think will happen if you do?

Adventure

Life is either a daring adventure or nothing at all.
Helen Keller

The theme of adventure permeates this phase of life for many of us. We may have followed the blueprint for living by cultural norms, or we may have pushed the envelope of those norms, but in either case we are ready to move beyond earlier limits and try something new. Some adventures are private, as we work on ourselves. Others are public, as we take on new work, play, relationships, and goals. Adventure embraces the unknown and accepts the uncontrollable. It acts anyway.

It's About the Journey

For as long as I can remember, I have wanted to grow. At first, I worked for better grades. As a teenager drawn to the life of faith, I strove to embody religious ideals. In young adulthood I aspired to success as a wife, mother, and professional. In midlife I embrace the challenge of aging with grace.

Our pragmatic culture typically defines wellness in terms of a healthy weight; success can be measured on the bathroom scale. Sometimes we add an exercise component to complete the picture. I have found, however, that health and happiness in midlife are much more complicated than that. Though physical fitness is still important, the golden years I long for go beyond sweating, starving, and servings of veggies per day.

My picture of genuine well-being portrays the capacity to enjoy life fully, to contribute, and to love well. I have learned to take personal responsibility and trust my power to change behaviors when I choose to. I see health as a robust interaction of mind, body, heart, and soul.

The journey through midlife has transformed my experience of well-being. Progress includes offering compassion to others when they annoy me. It involves spending more time on what matters most and less on trivial pursuits that clash with my deeper values. I rebound more quickly from setbacks. I respond more creatively to conflict. I center and focus more easily when frenzy threatens my peace of mind.

What does your midlife journey look like? How have you grown? What adventures are you planning for the months and years ahead?

Speaking and Dancing

I am stepping out of my comfort zone these days, and it surprises me. When I retired, I was so relieved! Now I could do the things I liked and stop doing things that made me uncomfortable. I never liked budget meetings: gone! Personnel actions: poof! Mandatory training: history!

I looked for smooth sailing (when I had a say). I knew I would face health issues, changing roles, and global warming. But, where I had a choice, I could stay in my comfort zone.

Then one day, something weird happened. I joined Toastmasters. Like most people, I dread public speaking. I had considered joining before, but never made the time to do so. Why now? I could easily avoid speaking in public these days, but I joined anyway. While it never became truly easy, I made noticeable progress. The comfort zone expanded, and I can speak more effectively now when I need or want to.

A year later, Lyle and I tried contra dancing. "Contra" is a good word, because this style of dancing runs contrary to everything that comes easily for me. Outside the comfort zone again, I fought to remember the difference between gypsy and swing, allemande and pass-through, partner and neighbor, left and right. I struggled with the intimacy of eye contact at close range, changing partners, and sweating with strangers. The comfort zone never really came into view, but each time was a little better than the one before.

In midlife I can see that the attraction of comfort is a trap: a trap I want to avoid. To be alive is to challenge the limits of what we think we can do. The alternative is a comfortable glide path to the end. Yes, I want to shift the balance toward things I love and away from things I don't. I also want to blur the boundary between them, and to move some activities from one category to the other by living life with a spirit of adventure.

Where does your comfort zone end and sense of adventure begin? What have you done to push your limits? What have you considered but postponed? Is this the time?

A Hundred Miles of Opportunity

That weekend I remembered once again why I am such a proud mom. For the second year in a row, our son Jonathan entered a hundred-mile race. For the second year in a row, he stopped short of the finish line. As he described it, "I want to run an ultra-marathon, and this one fits my schedule. Maybe I can't run 100 miles right now, but I will do as much as I can."

Why am I so proud? I am proud that Jonathan was mature enough in his mid-twenties to envision an ambitious goal, to train for that goal, and to test himself in public. He let us all know about his plans. He shared the outcome happily and without apology after choosing when to stop. Last year he finished 45 miles; this year he finished 62. For the latter, he received a silver belt buckle! Even race organizers acknowledge that 100 kilometers is worthy of applause in a 100-mile race.

On those occasions, Jonathan aimed beyond the assurance of success. He loved to run and enjoyed the motivation of training for a goal. He wanted to finish. He would have liked to win. He is also mature enough to know when both body and spirit are expended. He was willing to stop, adjust his definition of a happy outcome, and celebrate the results, whatever they were.

The goals we set take aim in different ways. They range from impossible dreams to baby steps in the right direction. The dream is a universe of opportunity. Training, effort, and a certain amount of luck determine how much of that opportunity we realize at a given time. I am learning from my son that achievements heading in the direction of the dream are victories, even when the original goal eludes our grasp.

What is your most ambitious goal? What have you done that leads you there, and how are you celebrating your progress? What will you do next?

Triumph in the Alps

I felt a surge of joy when Missoula ultra-runner Mike Foote's smiling face emerged from the darkness. When he crossed the finish line and wrapped himself in a Montana flag, tears welled up and my throat tightened. Foote had just claimed third place in a world-class field to finish the Ultra Trail du Mont Blanc (UTMB) in France. The event streamed live across eight time zones to the laptop in my living room.

The UTMB is a grueling adventure in the Alps. The numbers are impressive: That year, the race entailed 100 kilometers of mountain trail with thousands of feet up and down. The race began at 7:00 p.m. and the leaders finished at 6:00 the next morning. The entire event took place in the dark, in the wet, and in the cold. When an interviewer asked, "Why did you travel so far for this race?" Foote replied, "I came for the view."

I am an endurance-event junkie. I enjoy building my own modest capacity for distance, and I take inspiration from those whose potential carries them so much farther. The very names of bigger events give me goosebumps: The Hardrock. The Wasatch. The Bighorn. The Bear. The Western States. The Javelina. The JFK. I read the blogs, watch the videos, and ask to hear the stories again and again.

Athletic achievement serves not only as an inspiration in its own right, but also as a powerful metaphor for living life more fully. In life, as in sport, we are challenged to start with a finish line unimaginably distant. We keep moving through discomfort and pain. We run in the dark, navigating our headlight beam's limits and postponing concern for unknowns ahead. We flow with the unexpected, finding reserves of courage and resilience that we never knew we had.

I love watching my fellow humans run so far. It helps me believe that I, too, am built to last and that I will survive and thrive on the twists and turns of the path ahead, whatever they bring.

What tests of physical, mental, and emotional endurance have you faced? Have you taken time to celebrate your capacity to keep going, until the very end, no matter what?

Flying off the Cliff

It feels like Christmas when I see author Rick Hanson's periodic email, *Just One Thing,* in my inbox. Like a little kid, I rip it open with a mouse-click and dig out the gift inside. One recent morning the insightful essay was packaged with a bonus gift. Almost as an aside, Hanson shared the link to an extreme-sports video.

In a hurry as usual, I hesitated when I saw that it would take twenty precious minutes to view. Still, I trust Rick's judgment and clicked the arrow to start. The video clip featured a new sport in which riders ski off a precipice wearing a parachute. They alternate between skiing and flying to the bottom. The splendor of the setting, intensity of focus, and perfection of skill left me breathless and reflecting.

I get dizzy in steep country, and my terror of falling avoids slippery surfaces, steep slopes, and open air in any combination. Perhaps that is why I am drawn to those who make love with the demon I dread. In this video, Antoine Montant skis the challenging conditions and flies over impossible ones while hanging tight to the mountainside. In and out of touch, he reads the terrain with precision, engaging and releasing in turn.

I am intrigued by the implications of this sport for the adventure of everyday life. We are always, in some way, jumping off a cliff into open air. Just waking up confronts the slippery slope of a new day. Within a few recent weeks, I have been surprised by unexpected success, a trip to the emergency room, a wee-hours phone call, a life lost to cancer, and a friend's news of twins...dropping again and again off the precipice of life.

I jump into the day with eyes screwed shut and breath held tight. At best, I cling white-knuckled to the parachute and glide as far from the cliff as I can, maintaining distance from any possible point of impact. Rarely do I hug the cliff, touching down intentionally to experience the ride before lifting over another hazard on the path. I sense that those who confront their monsters up-close know them better and live with them in peace. I suspect they have less fear and more joy.

Antoine Montant died in October 2011 when his parachute failed. This intense young man followed his passion, perfected his talent, engaged closely with reality, and died in the arms of his beloved mountains. I wish as much for myself, for you, and for everyone we care for.

Let go of your fears and imagine flying for two minutes with Antoine. How does it feel? Can you picture this remarkable ride applying to your own life?

I Can Do It!

When asked to fill behind a manager who had retired, my initial response was guarded. I saw vast gaps in the skills I needed for the task. I envisioned more responsibility and a very real risk of failure. Self-preservation threatened to take over, and I almost declined the opportunity. When I look back on that experience now, I can see the lessons I have since learned about the ways in which we grow.

We often fall short of the knowledge needed to deal with a new situation. Looking at the crises other forest rangers had handled, I worried about employee grievances. I remembered angry hunters protesting a road closure. I dreaded a fatality on the fire-line. I did not know what I would say or do when it was my turn to lead in situations like those.

On a deeper level, however, I knew how to learn. As a toddler, I learned to walk. As a teenager, I changed my first flat tire. As a young adult, I learned with little warning how to make funeral arrangements, file insurance claims, and manage an inheritance. After long, hard thought I accepted the offer of a new role. I learned by trial and error, thrived, and took on even more responsibility as my career evolved. I draw strength from that long-past experience when life offers new challenges (and it does so every day).

We are continually bombarded with demanding circumstances, and in midlife the learning curve steepens. New health issues appear and results aren't always reassuring. Retirement arrives whether we are ready or not. Parents age and we want to help them while honoring other commitments in our lives.

There is always a gap when we face something hard for the first time. At those times we can tap into a lifetime of experience with learning and adapting under pressure. When we relive the obstacles we have overcome and the setbacks we have survived, we know deep inside, "I can do it!" And I do.

What past successes do you recall when performing under pressure? How do you leverage the skills of a lifetime when faced with something new?

Rear-view Mirror

I was waiting in Denver for the connecting flight back home. A dramatic lightning storm was passing through, and flights were delayed. As I reflected on the events leading up to this trip, I was amazed at the inner journey as well as the outer one.

Earlier in the year I had made Jane an offer, "I will run a half marathon with you for your 50th birthday, any time and any place you want." I didn't expect the Center of the Nation series but there it was, and I committed to something I didn't know that I could do.

As the months between promise and delivery progressed, I worried. When I added miles to weekly training, the twinge in my back acted up and one leg went numb from time to time. Other weak links threatened to join the party, and I wondered what I had been thinking. I run long every other week at most; this event called for 13 miles every other day. Would I use my Medicare card at some small-town emergency room before it was over?

But here I was in the airport, a shiny new multi-state medal around my neck. Looking back and feeling great, it was time to ask myself again: Why did we do it? What did we expect? What did we experience? We did it to honor a midlife friendship with shared adventure. We didn't know what to expect. Our experience was transformative.

During race week, we mingled with people from all over this country and others. Everyone had a story to share: the amputee running on a prosthetic leg; two men racing on rough roads with streamlined wheelchairs; the woman walking five full marathons in an orthopedic boot; the man raising money for Boston Marathon survivors; an elder boasting the shirt that read "50 marathons, 50 states, 9 times;" the smiling giant with a silver ponytail, hot pink t-shirt, matching calf-warmers, and a wife who volunteered all day, every day, all week.

The memories are as warm as the wind was cold. The memories of friendship fueled my desire for more. The sharing of challenges, the celebration of success both fast and slow, the smiling faces despite it all remind me that our responses to discomfort are a choice. My feet can hurt. My back can cramp. My fingers can burn with cold. But I can smile. I can shout out "Good job, Norm." And I can put one sore foot in front of the other until the very end. The joy might not look clear in the moment, but the focus sharpens in the rear view mirror.

When have you looked back on a tough experience and celebrated those very moments of pain, awkwardness, and failure that felt so bad at the time?

The Writer's Nest

I found it online several years ago, when searching for a vacation cabin. The tiny studio far from town was nestled in forest with a mountain view. It didn't meet our needs for a family reunion, but it looked like the perfect setting for a retreat.

I had been running too fast and scattering energy among too many priorities for too long. When the opportunity for time away came into view, I remembered the cabin. I had been working for six months on converting my weekly blog into a book. Bits and pieces of random progress were stuffed in my tote bag, crying out for concentrated and sustained effort. The experiment worked so well that I am eager to share the lessons I learned. They all had to do with creating a simple life, even for a few precious days.

The first day, I stocked up at the natural food store on simple ingredients and prepared dishes for the week. While I mixed up the food groups, I repeated the pattern from day to day. Oatmeal and applesauce. Hummus, raw veggies, and pita. Stir-fry with tofu and rice. Cold cereal with berries. Repeat.

Next, I set limits on social contact and entertainment. I checked email twice a day. I made only those phone calls needed for critical family ties. I did not try to figure out the satellite dish. I listened to calm meditation radio when silence demanded a change.

Each day I got up before sunrise and began writing. In addition to stopping for simple meals, I emerged from the nest each afternoon for a run, a hike, or a drive followed by a nap. Then I went back to writing until bedtime. When I drove down the mountain the next Sunday morning, my tote bag contained a printed first draft, tidy in its new 3-ring binder.

Since getting home from The Writers Nest, I have been working to apply the lessons I learned there to everyday life. I see opportunities to simplify my approach to food, manage the balance between outside stimulation and inner focus, and to break up periods of effort with exploration, activity, and rest. Whenever I remember how good it felt to practice these patterns in a less complicated setting, I treasure the spirit of a writer's retreat and hope to carry it with me wherever I go.

What is your experience with learning a new skill or gaining experience by going away, then bringing it home to enrich the rest of your life?

Caution on the Edge

Slow down. Construction ahead. Watch for flagger. Icy bridge. After a recent road trip, the images of signs like those are fresh in my memory. Likewise, a recent extreme-sports film festival brought the flip side of caution into focus. Extreme athletes find joy in the face-off with nature. They may also find death waiting for them there.

I tend to romanticize risk. That tendency pairs with an even stronger inclination toward caution. I drive to the mailbox on icy mornings, fearing another hard fall on concrete. I retreat to the treadmill when it is dark, windy, and wet. I check and re-check weather and road reports as departure approaches. I am, as a result, entranced by those who are skilled enough to thrive under harsh conditions. I seek to grow from their example, knowing that my degree of exposure to harm differs by an order of magnitude from theirs.

The ambiguity of facing and dealing with threat is captured in a phrase from *Running the Edge* by Tim Catalano, Adam Goucher, and Billy Mills. When writing about the journey to world-class competition, they refer to "the fine line between tough and stupid." They draw examples from their own lives to distinguish between the impulsive risk of a runaway ego and the calculated push beyond comfort needed to improve performance.

Adventure entails risk. It has an element of the unknown, and of facing things we can't control. It means stretching beyond the threshold of confidence to test our limits and improve our skills. It carries the real possibility of failure: freezing in the midst of a speech, relapse on the road to sobriety, rejection in the search for love, death on an alpine snowfield.

In reflecting on risk, I like the distinction between tough and stupid. Tough builds capacity in ambitious but calculated steps. Stupid counts on bravado to leap across the void. Tough sees the difference between soreness and injury. Stupid does not. Tough understands the implications of failure and accepts them. Stupid denies the implications and ignores them.

I welcome the example of extreme sports. We are capable of more than we think, and competence is built in the face of fear. I also honor the validity of caution signs along the road. It is smart to slow down in the tangled web of work zones. It is stupid to brake hard on an icy bridge. I can honor the warning signs, modify my approach accordingly, and continue moving ahead; or I can ignore them, proceed at full speed, and hope for the best.

Where in life do you take calculated risks? Where do you act on impulse when caution is called for? Where does fear impede the progress you want to make?

The Book Project

It was going so…very…slowly. At first I had thought it would be a snap. After all, the archives held more than 200 weekly *Reflections* essays to draw from. I could staple them together, add a cover, and "Voila!" the book would appear. The anniversary of that conclusion was only a couple of calendar pages away, and I was not there yet.

Early in the process, I had invited a small group of "book buddies" to share their impressions of my book as it evolved. What a diverse mix of creative folks I found! Whether it was a book title, cover design, or introduction, their commentary spanned a wide range of opinion. Consensus views were very helpful, but I was still learning how to work with those that diverged.

Another early step was to develop a framework of chapters that would sort random weekly topics into meaningful themes. That process was never-ending. As I sorted articles this way and that, I hit the mirrored walls of redundancy and fell into the abyss of significant gaps. Enough would eventually have to be enough. How would I know when that time had come? These and other challenges triggered the need to inquire, experiment, evaluate, and re-do.

As I paused for a moment to size up the effort that remained, I reflected on key lessons I had learned:

1. Writing a book does not take a direct route. It goes in circles that build into spirals that may advance, retreat, or veer off in a new direction altogether.

2. Learning cannot be rushed. A flash of insight bursts forth when least expected, lights a few steps, and goes out. The darkness can last a long time.

3. My writing is not really mine. It comes through me but not from me. Sometimes the Source flows, sometimes it babbles, sometimes it falls silent. I can encourage, but not force it to speak.

I am learning to trust that the process is its own reward. When I engage with an open heart and a willing spirit, the book project unfolds in its own way and on its own schedule. I am learning to let go and enjoy the ride.

What is your experience with projects that elude closure? How do you work with the energy of creative process, rather than fighting hopelessly for control?

Together on the Field of Play

Super Bowl Sunday and the Olympic Winter Games are all squished together this year. I love to watch skillful athletes putting forth their best effort, so I will spend the better part of three weeks glued to the TV in February. In addition to entertainment, I find that sport offers substantial grist for reflection. I am intrigued in particular by the unique blend of competitive opposition, team spirit, and good sportsmanship that arises when athletes align most truly with the tradition they represent.

Individual competition is always a factor when the best-of-the-best vie for world championship titles. Even team sports note record-setting individual performance and name their most valuable players. The spirit of competition expands to include communities of support that form around athletic success. We dress in the colors of our favorite teams and make bets with the other side. Governors square off, heads of state attend, and medal counts lead off many an evening newscast. As humans, our brains are wired to identify "us" vs "them" and to push one another out of the way in pursuit of competing interests.

Team spirit, while building on the opposition of my team vs yours, comes with the additional chemistry of cooperative effort. Athletic teams demonstrate that success derives from interdependence. While quarterbacks and captains draw individual acclaim for their leadership roles, they are quick to praise the efforts of others and to celebrate the accomplishments of the whole. As humans, we are designed not only to compete but also to work together for common goals.

Finally, good sportsmanship, the depth of character that can lose with grace and respect, offers another perspective on human spirit. Most competitors shake hands with opponents and mumble, "good job" after the game. Many add a sincere embrace and an honest smile of respect for the one who outperformed them that day.

This year the media reported an even more moving example of grace in defeat, when winning Seattle cornerback Richard Sherman told his post-Superbowl story. As he hobbled with a sprained ankle toward the post-game interview, he saw a hand reaching out toward his and heard losing Denver quarterback Peyton Manning ask how he was doing, how he felt. Sherman called that "one of the most incredible moments of my life." Another deeply human trait is altruism, the ability to care for someone else even when we ourselves are hurting.

I enjoy athletics on all three levels: the energy of competitive excellence, the power of teamwork, and the inspiration of altruistic good sportsmanship. I am moved to tears when an athlete who loses can reach out with genuine concern for another who won.

What do you find appealing in the world of sport? Where do you find it bringing out the best in those who play and those who watch?

Now We Are Three

It was late afternoon when a pair of weary hikers entered the visitor center where I worked. I heard a small squeaky voice before seeing the large fluffy cat with the amazing story. Tigger had approached the couple at a wilderness lake and followed them six miles back to their car. The shelter was already closed, so he came home with me for the evening. We woke to his mellow purring on the pillow between us. When he died 16 years later, we grieved.

Those years involved a lot of work travel and moving. We were busy parents to an active teenager. We also felt the vulnerable pain of losing a loved one. The decision was fairly easy: Any future pets would entail less care and looser bonding. Fish were fun, and, yes, we grieved when the silly upside-down catfish died. But we got over it faster, and flushing is quicker than burying.

During the second half of our married lives we have enjoyed the freedom of an empty litter box. But, over the past few months, something changed. I have been longing for a purring body on my lap and a chatty meow when I get home. Lyle has meanwhile been noting those symptoms with a tinge of alarm. While he loved Tigger and took care of him those many years, he appreciates the simpler life. Though I have promised that this time I will do the food and litter, he has every reason to question my follow-through. But it will be different this time. Really, it will.

I fell in love with her online picture, visited the shelter, and went shopping for supplies. Then before committing, I offered Lyle the chance to exercise his veto. Silence. Silence withholds enthusiastic approval. Silence preserves the option of saying that he told me so. Silence also, I have found over our years together, communicates mixed emotions, begrudging acceptance, and a willingness to try my most recent harebrained scheme.

Aspen is fluffy and chubby and terminally cute. She looks a lot like our beloved Tigger, which bridges to a happy past. She is calm and affectionate. She is diplomatic and knew enough to hop into Lyle's lap before gracing mine. She is curious and has a familiar tiny, squeaky voice.

It is a big deal to adopt a furry new child at this time in our lives. We are used to the comfortable emptiness of a pet-free home. I believe it is good for us to open our hearts and share our lives with someone new. I believe it is good for her to add a young and playful spirit to a quiet, loving home.

How have pets played a role in your life? Do you take special joy from the companionship of furry family members? How do the challenges balance out with rewards?

When Pigs Fly

In May 1964, I finished high school and left my hometown of Cincinnati, Ohio to embark on a lifetime of adventure in other places. This year I re-connected with my roots and sprouted a new branch of good memories there. I traveled to Cincinnati for the Flying Pig Half Marathon, an event that had been on my bucket list for more than a decade.

As I packed for the trip, I reflected on the tortuous and improbable path that had led me here. In high school, I was a full-blown nerd devoted to religious activities, Latin club, and yearbook. My single worst grade in four years of academic success was a barely-passing score in volleyball. If a crystal ball had shown me 50 years later, dressed in a cheetah-print miniskirt and running 13 miles, I would have returned it as defective and asked for a refund. When hell freezes over. When pigs fly.

Only a few exceptional women in my generation were physically active. Even fewer engaged in organized sports. I was clumsy and uncoordinated, overweight and friendly with the couch. The possibility that anything about that picture might change was beyond my ability to imagine.

Hiking the mountains of California during graduate school first broke the surface of my relationship with movement. Many years later, Lyle and I ran a 10K and my interest was piqued, but I quickly returned to the couch upon getting pregnant, and stayed there for 15 years. In my 50s, I cautiously returned to running as part of a weight-loss program. After a wild fling with the marathon distance, I settled into a long-term love affair with the half. The fitness that comes with distance training has been a genuine miracle, peeling off many effects of accumulating years.

Running also makes it clear on certain days that, in fact, the parts are aging. Lower back issues have tipped from intermittent toward chronic, and a pain in my knee flared up shortly before the Flying Pig. After consulting my diverse and supportive body-care team, I lined up with my pace group that Sunday morning and hoped for the best. More than three hours later, I claimed a finisher's medal with grateful joy.

I train for a running goal by building endurance in small steps over many months. I engage the power of a date on the calendar to counter fatigue, harsh weather, and the call of the couch. At this time in life, I also pray for the wisdom to hold that goal lightly, prepared to let go if the body says no. This year, I celebrated the improbable flights of many pigs over the past fifteen years, welcomed the chance for one more, and gave thanks that it did, indeed, include a finish line.

When in your life have pigs have flown against the odds? Do you remember to celebrate those times? How do you dance between committing to a goal and adjusting if conditions change?

Front and Back

Missoulian headline, July 14, 2014: "Sweltering Pace." The large photo of a 26-year-old athlete from Alaska, glistening with sweat and grimacing with effort as he won the Missoula Marathon, filled me with admiration and respect. Matt "Grizzly" Adams had just set a new course record of 2 hours, 22 minutes, and 27 seconds

New Haven Register headline, July 28, 2012: "Cheshire Marathoner Eugene DeFronzo Lapping the Nation." The large photo of a 76-year-old attorney from Connecticut, standing in front of more than 500 marathon finisher's medals displayed on the wall, also filled me with admiration and respect. This year he finished the Missoula Marathon in last place after 7 hours, 58 minutes, and 2 seconds.

Both men accomplished phenomenal feats of physical and mental endurance here last week. Both men covered 26.2 miles on foot. One made the cover of our local newspaper. The other was found in small print on the results page. I would like, here, to give Eugene DeFronzo a little more attention.

DeFronzo is memorable. His posture is contorted, his gait uneven, his expression purposeful. I first saw him in Park City, Utah in 2001 when I passed him on the last mile of my own first marathon. I found him again in 2013 at the Center of the Nation series, where he ran five marathons in five states in five days. His t-shirt there read: 50 marathons, 50 states, *nine times*. I noted the same face, pace, and shirt at the Flying Pig Marathon in Cincinnati in May. Then again this week. He shows up at a lot of marathons. It is what he does.

I admire and am inspired by people who challenge and expand their limits. I celebrate victories by young people who recognize and capitalize on innate athletic talents. I also celebrate the accomplishments of people at any age whose performance explodes the appearance of disability. The combination of training, effort, and perseverance required to finish a marathon is inspiring at any pace.

How do you see achievement in endurance events? Is speed the only measure of success, or can coming in last sometimes mean more?

Detour

Life is what happens to you while you're busy making other plans.
John Lennon

The best road trips have some of both: the well-planned and the unexpected. Detours happen when something goes wrong and we veer into the body shop, the emergency room, or the aging motel with "Vacancy" blinking in the window. The adventure of living has a similar mix of the intended and the serendipitous.

Times of Midlife Change

I envision midlife broadly as any stretch along the journey between birth and death. We are in the midst of living at any age; the only constant is change. Many years ago, I was given a bookmark with the words, "Life is what happens while you're making other plans." That phrase lighted my way through the pain of separation and divorce. It soothed my impatience during the search for satisfying work. Ever since, I have worked to accept the reality of unexpected change and to take responsibility for how I respond.

While we are making other plans or careening through midlife at full speed, our children leave home. Our parents need help. We fall in love with someone else. Our health takes a turn for the worse. Our finances dive off the cliff. We get a new boss, lose our job, or retire.

We have limited influence over the nature and timing of life changes. Yes, we can make plans. Yet even though we buy insurance, help the children shop for a college, and open an IRA, surprises wait around every bend.

I see the core work of midlife as building the skills to master the unexpected when it arises. The mastery I have in mind does not imply that we can control events, other people, or even ourselves. Mastery entails skillful engagement: riding the wave, skiing the fall line, and dancing to the music.

An example from my life may resonate with yours. In my forties I still had a childish temper. When things went wrong or people didn't behave as I wished, sudden anger sometimes erupted in screaming, slamming, and tears. The cycle was eventually transformed by spiritual writings that taught acceptance, inner peace, and unconditional love. I learned through reflection and practice to see the blessings hidden in events and people that irritated me.

I am a big fan of midlife and believe deeply in the grace that flows in times of change. We can build new skills to deal with pain. We can discard the patterns of denial and defensiveness that drag us down. We can draw upon our natural strengths, engage our networks, dig deep into our motivation, and make it all work better with the passing years.

What changes have shattered your world in the midst of living? What skills have you gained and how do you deploy them as life continues to happen?

Demons and Dead Ends

The message from Wes occupies an honored place in the sticky-gallery on my computer: "How we deal with failure is far more defining than how we deal with success." Like all of us some of the time, he had come through a tough week. Good intentions had evaporated in the heat of reality. The story is universal. It is the human condition. How, then, do we define ourselves in response?

Some setbacks originate within. They are the traits and habits that trip us up and prevent our progress. I call them demons. In *Tibetan Book of the Dead,* the path to rebirth is guarded by demons described in terrifying detail. The only way to move forward is to pass through those demons. The demons of our shortcomings likewise block the path to personal transformation. Only by facing them, going through them, and learning the lessons they teach can we move to the next level of living.

I personally host a herd of demons, such as those who rush to judgment. I strive for unconditional acceptance and compassionate respect, even when others are difficult and I am annoyed. Still, I am captured by the urge to criticize, to stereotype, and to come to harsh conclusions when someone falls short of my expectations. In moments of clear thinking, I can step back from judgment and appreciate the view through another's eyes. I can empathize and wish them well, then move beyond the demon and enjoy the day.

Other challenges arise from the outside events and circumstances that block our progress. I call them dead ends. Envision a maze with paths that work and those that don't. Only by trial and error do we find the continuous route that leads from entrance to exit. Setbacks on life's journey teach us to recognize dead ends and avoid them the next time through.

I often run into dead ends. I have a long list of goals and plans tacked to my mental bulletin board. Life often happens anyway. My fitness plan is derailed by weather or injury. The long-awaited vacation collides with a family crisis or work deadline. My inner four-year-old has been known to throw a fit when those changes pop up. My inner adult has been known to spray cool water on the flames and adjust to the new reality with grace. After many years of experience, I can make a smoother transition from rant to reality than I did earlier in my life.

Internal and external setbacks inflame. We want to make the trip from start to finish without a detour. We might get angry. We might give up. Or, we might decide to learn from the experience. Our choice defines the depth of our character, the quality of our journey, and the likelihood of reaching the destination we desire.

Name the demons and dead ends you have encountered recently. How have you responded? How would you like to respond differently the next time?

Asking for Directions

I encountered GPS technology for the first time at a family reunion far from home. Two relatives had cars with the "lady in a box," an electronic voice with an attitude who guided us to each destination. I especially liked her exasperated response when we missed a turn or chose an alternative route: "Re-calculating…"

On reflection, I see that the lady in a box speaks to more than finding motels and restaurants in a strange town. She reminds me of the larger journey of searching for the person I want to be and the choice-by-choice advice that guides me there.

A personal journey often begins with the destination in view. I commit to losing fifty pounds. I register for a marathon. I decide to reduce drinking or stop smoking. I promise better communication with the people I love most.

Each of these goals and others like them represent a major commitment to change direction and sustain purposeful effort over a period of months, or even years. Sometimes it works to swallow a big challenge in a single gulp. Often it does not. We really could use the lady in a box to keep us on track with small decisions turn by turn. We also need her when we overshoot or go the wrong way. It isn't always obvious, and our personal choices often veer off course: I join in when the group orders a second round of drinks; I turn off the alarm on long-run morning; I react with sarcasm, escalating a conflict that would have faded with silence. I jump into action without stopping to consider the consequences.

"Re-calculating."

As we mature on the journey, we attune more easily to our inner voice. We make fewer mistaken turns and recover more quickly. We know and trust the One Who knows what to say and what to do. The more often we ask for guidance and listen for the answer, the less often we retrace our steps to find the path anew.

How do you connect with inner guidance? How can you tell whether you are listening to the wise voice or an imposter before you decide to re-calculate?

Six Weeks in a Sling

I still remember the giddy joy I felt when the doctor told me to ditch the sling. The need for surgery had popped up without warning, and the process of recovery had offered a whole new and different learning curve than I had experienced before. Grateful that my "dominant hand" was still able to write, I kept a journal of challenge and change.

Entries for May begin with bold block lettering: "SURGERY!" A softer script goes on to suggest, *"Make lemonade out of lemons."* It expanded on the theme with: *"Less doing, more being. Less giving, more receiving. Less producing, more learning. Less independence, more interdependence."* The last was the most urgent, undeniable, and difficult for me.

Somewhere in early childhood I internalized the drive to do everything for myself. I shop at a grocery store where their customary offer to wheel food to the car triggers a self-righteous retort, "No thanks! I need the exercise." "Are you sure?" Yes, thanks." and then (silently) "Do I really look like a helpless old lady?"

The month after surgery generated quite a different response. Steering the cart, lifting the tailgate, and transferring bags from the basket were painful and help was welcome. I also enjoyed connecting with the helper as a person, finding out a little about them, wishing them well. I now see that accepting an offer of help can be as generous and kind as making such an offer in the first place.

Beyond the grocery store, opportunities to ask for and accept post-operative help abounded. As time passed, I began to appreciate the value of connection in new ways. I saw that strident independence can distance me from others. It also frees me from the implications of returning the favor. As I received help, I was better able to notice when someone else could use a hand. As I learned to accept help from others, I was inspired to offer support in gratitude for the many generous offers I had received.

What are your experiences with offering and accepting help in support of our interdependent human need?

Sight-shifting

Tiffany started teaching me the lesson several years earlier. As a member of our marathon training class, she had started in January to train for a long race six months away. After just a month, however, her legs rebelled. "Not this year!" they said. Without missing a step, Tiffany shifted her focus from training to support. She organized weekly water stations for the remaining months.

I was so inspired! I imagined that, in similar circumstances, I would withdraw entirely to avoid reminders of the goal I was forced to abandon. I did not think I could replace a performance goal with a service goal and enjoy it as much.

Then, this year, it happened to me. Grandma's Marathon in Duluth, Minnesota has been on my bucket list forever. When friend Mari and I looked for a perfect place to share her first half marathon, we decided on Grandma's. We won the lottery for an opportunity to register. Mike and Elaine offered us a place to stay. We trained and were ready to run.

Then, overnight, everything changed! A chronic shoulder injury turned acute. After surgery a week later, I was forbidden to run while in recovery. Good bye Grandma's. But what about Tiffany? She had showed me how to convert the passion for personal training into motivation for supporting someone else. With her example in mind I flew to Duluth anyway, enjoyed the visit with Mike and Elaine, and celebrated Mari's victorious smile at the finish line.

In the process, I learned a lesson about shifting sights. I love aiming at and preparing for goals of all kinds. Over the years I have struggled to be a good sport when the unexpected has changed my plans. This time, I learned not only to accept disappointment but to bounce back by setting a new goal. I also learned that the goal needn't be about me.

What are your experiences with sight-shifting? How have you re-focused your energy on new versions of success when life is "just a bowl of lemons" instead of cherries?

The Restart Button

In late January, Jane and I embarked on a three-month meditation class. Daily reading and prescribed mindfulness practice helped me develop a more peaceful outlook on daily life. After the formal class ended, however, I struggled to keep the habit alive.

Scientists report that it takes three weeks to start a habit and three months for it to become second nature, no longer requiring extra effort. My experience with meditation validates that finding. After three months, it felt natural to wake and spend twenty minutes focusing instead of hitting the to-do list at full speed. Then something changed.

I took a trip. My routine was disrupted. Waking up in motels meant going next door to Starbucks for caffeine. Waking up after I returned home meant unpacking, list making, grocery shopping, and re-entering the demands of a busy week. That was it for my new meditation practice, or so it seemed.

A month or so later I started meditating again. It felt awkward at first to sit quietly, focus the mind, and attend to the breath. In just a few weeks, second nature had turned back into extra effort. It wasn't easy, but I did it; I re-built the meditation habit and enjoyed the rewards.

Healthy new habits are like that. We start out with powerful intentions. We are motivated by novelty and early success. We establish a routine, and it becomes easier. Then something interrupts the pattern and we revert to earlier habits that don't serve as well. The gym membership lapses. Fruits and veggies rot. Fast food creeps back in. Maybe it is travel. Maybe it is soccer season. A string of back-to-back company. A change at work. A bad cold. Something will disrupt our new routine. It is easy to lose heart. The hard work of losing weight or training for an athletic goal, dedicating time for reflection or meeting weekly with a friend now seems to be lost.

With age, trial, and error I have gained confidence in restoring momentum. Having developed a habit that worked once, I can recall how good it felt to succeed and fire up the motivation needed to push the re-start button. I can tap into the knowledge that I made it happen before and that surely I can do it again.

How do you handle setbacks? Do you accept them as part of the adventure, or do you judge them as failures and use them as an excuse to give up completely?

More Questions than Answers

I am intrigued by the anonymous phrase, "Some years give us answers, while other years just raise the questions." The past year has been one of the latter, leading me on a search for answers while I struggled for composure around the unknown.

It started a few weeks after surgery. I developed a chronic and "gunky" cough and cleared my throat more often than usual, sometimes continually. As my voice hoarsened, public speaking and social conversation became awkward, and I pulled back from situations that called for talking. Running and other physical activities generated more coughing; it got better when I sat quietly in one place. I drifted uneasily toward a more solitary and sedentary lifestyle.

Hours of online research, multiple medical screenings, and advice from diverse practitioners produced little in the way of answers. I am grateful that many life-threatening conditions have been ruled out, but the annoyance remains unsolved. The process of testing the less frightening theories is time-consuming and far from conclusive.

I do not expect unanswered questions in the 21st century. I am used to quick fixes. I expect a pill that relieves symptoms, at least for a while. Not in this case. I am frustrated by theories that are diametrically opposed and treatments that are mutually exclusive. I am caught in a frenzied search for relief that spins in circles and goes nowhere in particular.

I am grateful that, for all the questions, the answers so far are benign. It does not appear as if my next lesson is learning how to die. It may, however, be learning to live joyfully and peacefully with discomfort and uncertainty. It is a time for questions not for answers.

I know I am not alone. I know you share these experiences. How do you deal with them?

Choose Life

She was only 57 when she received the impossible news. Pancreatic cancer. She was young and vibrant, healthy and wise. Only a few people knew about the abdominal pain. Now we all knew. We recoiled in disbelief. We shook to the roots and sobbed with bottomless denial, anger, bargaining. Acceptance? No! Way too soon for acceptance.

A few months later, we sat together in her living room. Kerry had asked me to be her life coach. She expressed herself in terms unique to the beauty of her soul, describing life as a continuum between living and dying. "We are all somewhere on the continuum," she said. "We have a choice," she said. "I want to focus on the living end of the continuum." For fifteen months between diagnosis and departure, Kerry repeatedly chose life. The photos from her son's wedding show a proud mom bursting with joy. She went to Hawaii. With a granddaughter on the way, she wrote a book about grandmothers.

She started a blog, and called it "Kerry's Project." It displays remarkable views from the journey. We join her at Johns Hopkins in Baltimore, where she validated the initial opinion. We meet her team at MD Anderson in Houston, where she joined in a clinical trial. We get to know her family and friends, featured in intimate stories from decades of living and loving. We share her commentary on stages of living with death in the viewfinder.

Kerry struggled with the fact that we, her loved ones, started to grieve before she was ready. While she made a daily effort to choose life, we often succumbed to our own fears and sense of loss. Each of us looked for a way to help, to offer what was needed, not to get in the way, not to overwhelm, not to make her story a story about us.

The day came when we knew it was our last visit. Life would soon pass her along to the next adventure. I asked if there was anything I could do. She asked if I would "say something nice" at the memorial service. I teased that it would be hard to think of something nice. I was deeply touched that she asked. At last, there was something I could do to help. It didn't work out that way. I was a thousand miles away. I wrote some nice things and sent them to her family, to be used as they wished. I thought about her all that day and felt that she was very near.

The gifts of sharing that year with Kerry continue to be precious. I learned that it is not denial to choose life with a diagnosis of terminal cancer. It is making the most of what-is and letting go of what-is-not.

What is your experience of dancing with dying? How has it changed your view of the choices we face at the end? Of the choices we face every day?

Missions, Malfunctions, and Miracles

I had cut it too close. I usually draft my weekly *Reflections* essay by Wednesday, allowing for several editing cycles before posting on Sunday morning. That time, Saturday dawned with nary a word on the screen, and worse yet, nary an idea in mind. It felt like playing hooky when, instead of heading home from the farmer's market to write, I turned the other way.

My hometown is surrounded by its own ring of mountain scenery, but less than an hour to the north is an even more spectacular view of the Mission Range. A scenic overlook along the highway is one of my favorite places to stop, read, listen to music, and savor the beauty. I hoped those moments of inspiration would offset the hours away from a keyboard. When they ended, however, the story behind that week's issue of *Reflections* had just begun.

I turned the key in the ignition to head back home, but nothing felt or sounded right. The engine was running, but I pressed the accelerator to little effect. The car inched out of the parking space, and then inched back in. A tight ball formed in my stomach. My heart raced, breath shortened, and mind went blank. Forty miles from home, five miles from the nearest town, my cellphone charge was low and I had no clue what to do next.

A couple from Nevada had also stopped at the overlook and asked if I was OK. After checking under the hood and speculating about possibilities, they followed me at a snail's pace to town. They helped me find a garage and resumed their travels only after knowing I had found the assistance I needed. The garage owner guided me kindly through the options for dealing with a dying car. His son drove me back to Missoula and made sure I had lined up another ride before leaving me alone. They went an extra mile, again and again.

When I sat down at last to write, I was at home. I was safe. I was comfortable. I savored the beauty. Morning had begun with the beauty of nature: snowy peaks, green hills, and a sunny sky. Afternoon added the beauty of human kindness: generous strangers helping in my time of need. The former was expected; the latter was a surprise, a gift, and a miracle.

What is your experience of help freely given when most needed and least expected to appear?

I Feel Your Strength

In a miracle of serendipity, the new book on my shelf during a month dense with setbacks was *Bouncing Back*, Linda Graham's marvelous treatment of resilience. Graham draws on research that explores the interplay of neuroscience, relational psychology, and meditative practice to help us understand and improve our responses to unexpected and unwelcome events in our lives.

Graham sees a central role for empathy in dealing with change, and tracks that role to the brain. Empathy arises from the activity of mirror neurons, which enable us to resonate with the mental and emotional states we encounter in others. You feel my pain as if it were your own. You reach out and help. Empathy surrounds me with kindness and helping hands.

Mirror neurons have yet another function in times of need. Not only do they help us identify with one another's pain and respond helpfully, they also help us share our strength and competence, increasing the ability of those who suffer to cope. When I feel helpless, I can resonate with your confidence and grow in my own. On the other hand, when you convey despair, I may give up before I begin.

I worked my way through divorce by spending time with a friend who had managed her own separation with grace and skill. I resonated with the calm confidence and peace of mind she conveyed. In contrast, I confided in another friend when my mother was diagnosed with cancer. That friend had lost her own mother to a similar condition, and the depth of her grief infected me too. When I tuned into her emotional wavelength, I internalized her hopelessness and my capacity to move forward took a turn for the worse.

Understanding the empathic impact we have on one another can help us both to overcome our own misfortune and to respond appropriately when others face hard times. When I struggle, I can seek out people who convey reasonable optimism and who can see my underlying ability to recover. When I want to help another, I can shape my response to bolster their resilience. While acknowledging their pain, I don't add my own emotional baggage or convey a feeling of hopelessness. I provide a strong shoulder that they can first cry on, then lean on as they stand tall and move ahead to deal courageously with their lives.

Can you remember when a friend responded to your problem with positive empathy? How did it feel to gain strength from her confidence in you and faith in the outcome?

A Time and a Season

Each year in July, my hometown hosts the Missoula Marathon. For each of the past few years, that day has capped off a six-month training class that I coach. We use Jeff Galloway's trademarked "run-walk-run" approach to distance and appeal in particular to newer, older, and injury-prone runners. We help people prepare for a goal that many never imagined possible.

Each year, most class members meet the goal in July that they set in January. They run the race. They cross the finish line. They receive a medal. Their names and times are listed in the results. They post pictures. They celebrate with family and friends.

Each year, other class members fall short of the success they envisioned at the beginning. They are injured or sick. Their families need them. They cannot take the day off from work. I have written already about shifting our sights when circumstances change. Those who cannot run on race day often shift their sights to support their peers. They cheer on the sidelines, distribute race packets, or hang finishers' medals around sweaty necks.

As their training program coach, I am as proud of the second group as the first. Every single class member has risen to the midwinter challenge of testing themselves against the prospect of running long distances. Each member has come through a unique personal journey. Each member has contributed in his or her own way to the journeys of others. It has been a remarkable individual effort, and an even-more remarkable collective effort.

I am reminded of the verse from Ecclesiastes, and the tune added much later by Pete Seeger. "To everything (turn-turn-turn) there is a season (turn-turn-turn), and a time for every purpose under heaven."

A time to learn and a time to test. A time to hurt and a time to heal. A time to fall and a time to rise. A time to cry and a time to smile. A time to love and be loved; to help and be helped.

For those of us who follow Jeff Galloway's trademarked approach to running, there is also a time to run and a time to walk. I celebrate a remarkable season of building endurance and community one week and one mile at a time.

Which of your goals have jumped off the tracks this year? What comes next?

Holy Days

In his 20s, Jim was diagnosed with an inherited kidney disease. Shortly after losing his own father, he learned that he carried the same gene. We bonded with Jim the year he placed his daughter's hand into that of our son and blessed their union. It was the same year that he qualified for a kidney transplant.

Jim and Mari, Lyle and I formed a warm bond at the wedding and enriched that bond by sharing a number of trips. We celebrated anniversaries and graduations. We played tourist. We laughed and told stories. We so enjoyed the unexpected gift of friendship that came with the merging of our family histories.

Less than four years into the new friendship, we honored Thanksgiving with gratitude for a successful kidney transplant. We held our breath over Christmas, as Jim returned to the hospital with complications. We wept at year's end when the happy ending turned sad.

It was difficult to respond when cheerful friends asked, "How were your holidays?" The question inevitably triggered memories of hope, hope dashed against the rocks of reality, pain, and loss. But that was not all that it triggered.

When I reflected on the New Year, I also remembered the beauty of family gathered in loving embrace. I thought of those who came from far away and those who were stymied by weather. I remembered the beauty of flower arrangements, family photos, and mementoes on display. I remembered the celebration of an ordinary life lived in an extraordinary way.

I thought of the strong women—wife, daughters, mother, sister, aunts and nieces—whose pain reflected the depths of their bond and the role Jim had played as the man in an extended female family. And, among those women, I remembered best the woman who spoke on behalf of them all.

Jennie gave the eulogy at her father's funeral Mass. She spoke with calm and grace, unscripted and from the heart. The stories she told flowed with humor and affection. This was the Jennie who loves our son and belongs to our family, too. This was the Jennie who brought Jim and Mari into our lives and introduced us to a man whose loss we now grieve.

How were the holidays? They were painful. They were complicated. They were filled with both loss and love. They were beautiful. And they were holy.

The price of love is the pain of loss. You have no doubt experienced that fact as well. Where do you find the impetus to move forward, to heal, and to love some more?

Perspective

Some people are always finding fault with Nature for putting thorns on roses; I always thank her for having put roses on thorns.
Alphonse Karr

I was well into adulthood and still given to meltdown when life didn't go my way. Then one day a casual conversation started me on the path to profound change. Beginning with the spiritual text, *A Course in Miracles,* and leading from there to decades of related reading and practice, I have gained immeasurable perspective on events, emotions, and action. I can usually view the most upsetting circumstance from a different angle that opens to compassion, acceptance, and creative response.

Serenity, Courage, and Wisdom

God, grant me the serenity to accept the things I cannot change, the courage to change the things I can, and the wisdom to know the difference. (Reinhold Niebuhr)

Like many others, I tend to over-react when events don't go my way. A recent confrontation with back pain demonstrates the point. At first I resisted the evidence and beat the walls of my personal prison with denial and outrage. I resented the weak physical link that disrupted my plans. Eventually, getting nowhere, I asked for the serenity to accept the things I could not change. When I stopped fighting the truth, I was able to explore realistic options with an open mind.

The prayer does not, however, stop with acceptance. It moves on to ask for *the courage to change the things I can*. Just as I sometimes resent circumstances that are outside my control, I also succumb to helpless whining when I really could make a difference. I despair in the face of intractable habits: "I just can't stick to a healthy plan and lose those twenty pounds." I complain about the government: "Why don't they stop playing politics and get something done?" I complain about others in my life: "My boss is a jerk, giving me a project she knows I will hate." Are situations like these really beyond our control?

Sometimes *the wisdom to know the difference* suggests that I take a closer look. If I want to change an unhealthy habit, I must try something different the next time. I will ask for the courage to do so. If I want to influence the civic process, I must get involved. I will ask for the courage to do so. If I want to challenge the work assignment, I must express myself honestly and constructively. I will ask for the courage to do so.

I may decide, after all, that I am not willing to make the effort needed to change the situation at hand. In choosing not to act, I relinquish the right to complain and I pray for the serenity of knowing that I had a choice, and chose to let it go.

What are the dilemmas between serenity and courage in your life? How do you distinguish between things you cannot change and those that you can?

Future and Presence

Goals are fun. They are motivating. They enliven our time with a sense of purpose. Goals are also a trap. They set us up for all-or-nothing thinking and they can blind us to the need for changing priorities. Today I want to explore the challenge of living in harmony with long-term goals, aspiring to a better future while living fully in the present.

Both spiritual and psychological teachers recommend the practice of presence, of attending to what is happening in the moment. Spiritual writer Eckhart Tolle calls it *The Power of Now*. Psychologist Mikhail Csikszentmihalyi calls it *Flow*. Inner peace and optimal happiness do not arise from chasing tomorrow's goals.

Why then, as a proponent of happiness, do I advocate the practice of goal-setting? When I dig for an answer to that question, I find that goals reside not only in the future. More importantly, they offer a framework for living more deeply in the moment. When I set a goal, I connect with the inner wisdom that knows what is most important. My most powerful desires for the future are built upon the intentions and values I hold sacred today.

I have a goal of physical health, but why is it important? I want to have the strength and energy to make a contribution. I want to invest in travel and learning, not in medical bills. I want to live a long time in my elder-unfriendly home and care for its labor-intensive yard. I want to actively enjoy my son's adulthood and welcome the possibility of another generation. As a step toward embodying those deeper values, I set goals for eating, exercise, rest and recovery that lead me where I want to go.

Goals are most powerful when they arise from present values. They are most rewarding when they add purpose and direction to our choices in the moment. Goals distract us from the present when they shift our focus to the future and divert attention from the path we are walking today.

Take a look at your own plans and promises. Are they grounded in the present? Do they guide your choices and energize your action in the now?

In Exile or at Home?

I have long loved arid places, and in particular enjoy the weird and wonderful adaptations of desert plants. Along a winding path in the Desert Botanical Garden in Phoenix, I read this thought-provoking observation on an interpretive sign: "The most significant lesson that desert dwellers can learn is to regard themselves not as exiles from some better place but as people at home in an environment to which life can be adjusted." (Forrest Shreve, botanist)

The message in that quotation struck close to home. It was November, and just a few days earlier I had written from home in Montana about the effect of dreary weather on my mood. Perhaps the most significant lesson that desert dwellers can learn is one that applies to us all. When the sky is gray and pavement wet, I may regard myself as an exile from the better place of sunnier times. Or I can make myself at home by adapting to the here and now.

I find a similar pattern when engaging with the emotional environment. I may feel lonely or bored, overwhelmed or anxious, irritable or depressed. Do I regard myself as an exile from a better time of easier happiness, or can I make myself at home with these perceptions and emotions? Am I trapped, or can I adapt?

I believe in the power of adaptation, not only on a biological level but on a mental and emotional plane. We can choose to sink under the weight of dark times, or take steps to work with what we are given. Inspiring reading, beautiful music, connecting with happy memories, reaching out to others, engaging in creative outlets all provide ways to be "at home in an environment to which life can be adjusted."

Are you living in exile from a better time? A better place? A better job? A better relationship? Or, are you adapting to the challenges of today?

Doors and Windows

"Whenever the Lord closes a door, somewhere He opens a window." That observation, attributed to Mother Superior in *The Sound of Music*, came to mind as I reflected on recent events. Just after returning from travel, desperately behind on several important projects, I despaired when the computer died. After five years of flawless service, it began to require two, three, and even five attempts before booting into consciousness. The technician at the computer store confirmed my hunch. It was on the way out. The door was swinging shut.

Driven by deadlines, I sped through the stages of grief, accepted reality, and bought a new machine the next day. Windows opened. Windows 8. Microsoft's most recent experiment in patience and persistence.

Windows 8 and its friends, the "Apps," demonstrated an endearing desire to please. In the process, they tripped all over themselves, anticipating my every wish (and mostly getting it wrong). With fingers hovering over the touchpad, I contemplated the next step while the computer guessed what I wanted. Without my asking, it shifted spontaneously from screen to screen. From gigantic font to microscopic. From the last task I was working on, to what I might do next. Charms. Widgets. Buttons. They appeared quickly and even more quickly vanished. It drove me crazy.

This is not the kind of window I expected to open when the door closed. I expected a clear, clean window with an unobstructed view. I expected logic. I expected help. Instead, I got this. I registered for a class on the spot, and prayed for the time to fly by. In the interim, I struggled to produce results on tight timelines while learning the new system intuitively. Aaack.

I love technology. I hate technology. It does so many things well. It does too many things well. It makes life simpler. And more complex. I was caught in the conundrum. I needed to stop. I needed to re-frame my goals and my deadlines. I needed to read the instructions. I needed to ask for help. I couldn't go on as if nothing had changed.

Whether or not the hand of God was evident, the Vista door had closed and Windows 8 had opened. It did not, however, open all the way, and I banged my head against the frame as I struggled to move forward. I hope to remember the next time that panic does not help; a cool head and steady focus do. When I stop, breathe, and take one step at a time, solutions to impossible dilemmas gradually appear.

How do you handle a new learning curve when time is short? What helps you settle down enough to chart a path through confusion to competence?

Dream and Nightmare

I was so proud of myself! I had navigated the complexity of online streaming and thrilled to the tight finish of men's and women's competition. I had found my friend on the web, and tracked his progress to the finish line. I had gone on to other things, but left Boston Marathon coverage on the screen, running in the background, connecting me with USA road running's annual signature event.

I have dreamed of Boston ever since beginning to run fifteen years ago. It is the one major distance race that requires participants to qualify in advance. It has been awhile since I seriously considered that possibility, but like the live online coverage, it runs in the background of my awareness. Each time a friend qualifies, I feel a vicarious surge of pride and joy.

Then, on the third Monday of April 2013, something changed. I glanced at the screen between chores and saw an odd cloud of smoke billowing out from the left side of the picture. I spent the rest of the day, numb with disbelief, watching the coverage. Online, we runners expressed the full range of emotion: horror, anger, defiance, prayer, compassion, sorrow, fear, and relief that our own loved ones were OK.

I debated whether to reflect in writing on the Boston bombing. What can I say that hasn't been said? Which perspectives do I want to internalize and share? Whatever the answers to those questions, I cannot leave the topic behind. As a runner, I cannot evade this pivotal experience in the history of our sport. Boston the dream is now tinged with Boston the nightmare.

It feels extraordinary, but isn't that, in life, always the case? In my dream, some times and places are sacred and safe from harm. In my nightmare, nothing is certain and safety is relative. Horrible things happen: acts of nature, acts of humans. They shake our world and remind us how vulnerable we are. Is there, then, no refuge?

I find refuge in the community of response to suffering when it occurs. I grow from the experience of watching emergency teams in action. I am inspired by the messages of compassion and support that proliferate. I am uplifted by the courage and depth with which victims overcome their anguish and move on to live again.

The dream of a pain-free life is an illusion; all lives are tinged with nightmares. The nightmare need not, however, have the final say. We can help and we can ask for help. Our spirits are resilient and our communities are supportive. Morning comes eventually and we awaken to a better day.

What insights and perspectives help you deal with the tragedies in your own life and the lives of others?

How Full is Your Glass?

Dead on the road. Cancer. Blizzard on the pass. Those of us with a tendency to envision worst-case scenarios such as these can blame our ancestors. A bias toward hope or toward gloom is found in our genes; my grandmother was a world-class worrier, and so am I. I fabricate catastrophes if a loved one is late coming home, a suspicious symptom appears, or the weather forecast threatens my plans.

The painful habit of imagining the worst led me to *Learned Optimism*, by psychologist Martin Seligman. The author makes a compelling case for the hopeful view. Optimists are happier than pessimists because they interpret the events in their lives in positive terms. Optimists are healthier without the stress of chronic fear that leads to disease. Optimists are more successful because high energy fuels their effort, while the energy of a pessimist drains with the expectation of failure.

Fortunately, Seligman moves beyond the implications of inherited tendencies to propose an alternative for those of us inclined to worry. In *Learned Optimism*, he urges us to change our perspective by adopting thought patterns from positive peers.

Pessimists see setbacks as permanent; I interpret knee pain as a sign of decline. "What can I expect at my age? Maybe I should stop running." I can re-frame my perspective like the optimist whose pain is a bump in the road; "With some ice and physical therapy, I'll be back in no time."

Pessimists register one event as a sign of something bigger: "It sucks getting old. Today it's my knee, tomorrow something else. I'm falling apart at the seams." Optimists, in contrast, see problems as exceptions to the rule. "That knee has sometimes been tricky, but I am healthy and strong. As long as I listen to my body, I can do most anything I want."

Finally, pessimists blame adversity on intrinsic personal flaws, while their glass-half-full counterparts attribute the same events to outside forces. The optimist steps in a hole, twists her ankle, chalks it up to happenstance, and moves on. Her pessimistic friend calls herself a klutz and expects to fall in every hole that comes along.

Pessimism is not just unpleasant; it also affects the outcomes in our lives. Those of us who expect the worst tend to find it. We do not have the positive energy to learn from experience and rebound from setbacks as well as those with a more positive slant. I am pleased to know how to change the response I inherited by choosing a better way.

Where do you see yourself on the spectrum between hopeless and undaunted? How do you create a more hopeful view when nature holds you back?

Thank You for Being a Pain

A few years ago, I discovered a creative twist around the benefits of giving thanks. In *Worst Enemy, Best Teacher*, Deidre Combs describes brain studies that show we cannot experience gratitude and fear at the same time. As we work to develop more optimism and defuse the effects of chronic anxiety, the habit of gratitude is a powerful ally. The perspective of appreciation can be cultivated in untroubled times and deployed when needed to cope with adversity.

Any perception of threat enters the brain through the senses and proceeds to the neurological dispatch center for emergency response. Instinctive responses are limited to three: freeze, fight, or flee. If we pause before those impulses kick in, we can engage the rational brain, dilute fear and anger, re-interpret the threat, and seek a creative solution. In the architecture of the brain, gratitude and creative response are side by side: when we give thanks, fear retreats and wisdom can take its place.

Another recent read takes the theme a few steps farther. *Thank You for Being Such a Pain*, by Mark I. Rosen, explores the role of difficult relationships in personal growth. Rosen suggests responding to conflict with gratitude and following up with creative response. "Thank you for being such a pain, I can learn a lot from you."

Imagine an irritating remark (the kind that could trigger a dramatic exit and a slamming door). Now imagine yourself responding instead with "Thank you." Envision in that phrase the portal to a different way of seeing. "Thank you; I hadn't thought of that." "Thank you, I will take that into account." "Thank you; I can always use a reminder." If Deidre Combs is right, the next sentence may lead us creatively beyond striking out or running away.

When has a person who was being a pain transformed your view? Did you thank them then? Do you want to thank them now?

Ordinary Lives

Lyle and I were married over Columbus Day weekend. Not only did we have an extra day off, but it coincided nicely with Lyle's birthday the following day. Ever since, we have found this lovely mid-autumn holiday a special time to reflect and celebrate. We remember the gifts of life and committed love, and honor the progress we have made.

Anniversaries and birthdays are recurring mile markers along life's path. We make a big deal over birthdays ending in zero and those silver, golden, and diamond anniversaries. But for the most part, each occasion simply marks "one more year" and "better than the alternative."

In both cases, each additional year is indeed a big deal. We celebrate the ordinariness of our lives and the value of getting up every day and choosing: choosing life, choosing relationship. Another birthday means we have been looking in the mirror at more wrinkles, age spots, and perhaps scars than ever before. The anniversary means looking across the table at an older, grayer, and perhaps less romantic version of the person we fell for so many years ago.

Our popular culture does not make a habit of appreciating the everyday. Even less does it celebrate decline. We Americans are all about progress, youth, and change. New and improved. Faster. Bigger. Better than ever.

Maybe the ordinary birthdays and anniversaries are, in a way, counter-culture. They reward perseverance. They celebrate the fact that we show up and keep going, like the hundred-mile runners I admire and occasionally write about. Whatever the terrain, we keep going. Whatever the weather, we keep going. Whether or not it feels good at the moment, we keep going. For better or worse. Richer or poorer. In sickness and in health.

We don't generally get faster with age. Or stronger. Or healthier. Or more beautiful. Or more passionate. Or, even, wiser (though I hope at least for that much). We either resign ourselves to a chronic sense of failure, or we make it a point to celebrate endurance for its own sake.

Are you disheartened by the passage of time? Do you fidget at the sameness of your life? I urge you to celebrate the ordinary gifts of life and love, however well-disguised they may be.

Wedding and Funeral

Within a 10-day span, I attended the wedding of dear friends and watched Senator Ted Kennedy's funeral on television. Events such as these are sacred, in part, because they call us to celebrate the best and look past the rest.

A wedding looks forward with promise. It challenges the love of two people to last, to hold them together in committed partnership. The Scripture for this wedding proclaimed that love is patient and kind; it is not ill-mannered or selfish or irritable. It never gives up. Its faith, hope, and patience never fail. In marriage, we promise to stay through better and worse, richer and poorer, sickness and health, 'til death do us part.

A funeral looks backward when, in fact, death has indeed parted us. The celebration of life at a funeral calls to mind a person's virtues, tenderness, and sense of humor. Person after person lauded Senator Kennedy for his commitment and perseverance. He never gave up on causes that he believed in. He let go of life reluctantly, regretting the unfinished work he left behind. Differences, no longer relevant, were set aside as allies and rivals alike remembered the good. Flaws and setbacks faded into the background.

Both weddings and funerals are occasions for hope. They focus on the best we have to offer, whether looking forward or looking back at a lifetime of shared experience. They acknowledge the tough times and affirm that those tough times are given us to transcend and to be transformed. Life's journey, love's journey, and our own journeys: they are all about focusing on what is important and putting the rest in perspective.

Imagine the end of your life. Loved ones are gathered. How do you want to be remembered? Does your life today embody your ideals? Is it time to renew your vows?

To Celebrate or Not

I think I caught a twinkle in his eye. "Really? Do we celebrate those anymore?" I had just raised the subject of what we might do on my birthday this year. My resounding answer was "Yes!"

Yes! I am always scanning the horizon for excuses to play, to launch an adventure, to eat and drink something special in a new place. My birthday is well suited to celebration, coming in midsummer when outdoor opportunities abound. It usually includes a trip or a hike, and always a component of ice cream and beer. Of course we celebrate our birthdays! Why not?

When I look around, I see that some people say, "No." Birthdays are for children. Don't make a fuss over me. I don't need any more things. My favorite foods are all off-limits these days. Most of all, I don't want to acknowledge the accumulation of years. I don't want others to know, and I don't want to admit how old I really am.

Sixty-six. It was a big number that year (and has grown since). The lives of my parents ended much earlier than that. News reporters describe my age group as "elderly." All of the senior discounts lie within my grasp. My AARP card is yellowed and frayed with age; even the Medicare card shows signs of wear. Body parts grumble, "Nothing lasts forever." However, Yes! I do still celebrate my birthday. It is about more than the hike, the ice cream, and the beer. Above all, I celebrate the gift of life and thank those who made it possible.

I celebrate my parents, who had married secretly and for whom my appearance blew their cover. They welcomed me anyway. My father, at 48, did not expect another child. He bought me a football before I was born and cradled me anyway. As a young widow and single parent, my mother was tempted to hold me close, but she sent me away to college anyway.

I celebrate my husband and our son, who have provided a supportive family circle since my mother died. Lyle and Jonathan (and now Jennie) are my emotional base camp of safety and support. I celebrate the friends who provide a loving network of encouragement.

I give thanks for the wisdom teachers who help me see life as a meaningful journey. I celebrate the Higher Power from whose generous hand my life emerged on earth so many years ago. Yes I want to celebrate! I want to take a hike, have dinner at a new restaurant, and stop by a new craft brewery on the way home. And, of course, I want ice cream to top it all off!

How do you like to celebrate your birthday? And why?

Getting Into It

He dangled from the cliff on a rope, swinging to and fro without a clue what to do next. The helpful young instructor below asked what was happening. He replied, "I don't want to talk about it." She then shared a motto from Outward Bound, the adventure leadership program in which he was enrolled: "If you can't get out of it, get into it." That story from author Parker Palmer bubbles up from the back of my brain whenever I need it most. I need it now.

I have written elsewhere about my increasing struggle with throat congestion. It is not a pretty topic. It is not serious. It is not life threatening. But it is seriously annoying. From doctor to doctor, test to test, and experiment to experiment nothing conclusive has come forth. I seem to be destined for a future encumbered with throat-clearing, coughing, and chronic laryngitis. It took me a year or more to realize that I probably can't get out of it. There is no quick fix. There may not be any fix. If I want to get out of it I must get into it, taking the tough steps needed to mitigate symptoms and to live in peace with those that remain.

I have also periodically reflected on helping Lyle's parents as they age. For the longest time, things went well. The folks had more good days than bad, and the bad days were tolerable. When we visited for a week at a time, we saw remarkably vibrant people living their 80's in style. Then, somewhere along the way, the balance shifted. Bad days caught up with the good days and passed them by. We began to see, even during short visits, that their needs were growing. We struggled to acknowledge, and struggled harder to respond. Now we are struggling to know what helps.

Each month, I choose a few themes for personal growth. The themes for this month are family and health. In those two areas of my life, I want to stop trying to get out of it and to get more deeply into it. In doing so, I can support Lyle's desire to spend more time with his parents by finding others to help with yard work and snow removal when he is away. I can work with laryngitis by monitoring my conversation and public speaking and backing off from speaking before the irritation worsens.

I suspect that your life also has challenges that defy resolution. Where does the motto "If you can't get out of it, get into it" fit for you?

Living with Joy

The title captured my attention, and the review pulled me in. One click later, *Until I Say Good-bye* found a place in my Kindle library. Since then, underlying messages from the memoir by Susan Spencer-Wendel have pervaded my perspective on life and pain, disability and death.

Diagnosed with ALS (Lou Gehrig's disease) at the age of 44, the young reporter and mother of three took on the project of documenting her experience and sharing it with others. The story of preparing to say goodbye could be maudlin. It could be gut-wrenching. It could pass over reality to paint a happy face on a sad scene. But it does not.

The subtitle of Spencer-Wendel's book completes the sentence: *My Year of Living with Joy*. As she types the memoir with one thumb on her iPhone, the author takes us on a remarkable journey from Florida to Budapest to Greece, from adulthood to infancy and back, from denial to acceptance and beyond to the celebration of life, however long or short it may be.

I am terrified of pain. I am terrified of losing the ability to function in any number of ways. While I fear the unknown of dying as well, the prospect of living with challenges like those described in this book tempts me to view death a better option. The author's love of life, however, turns that fearful perspective upside-down.

More than three years after diagnosis, Susan Spencer-Wendel recently said good-bye. People around the world had read her book, felt the loss, and gave thanks for her life. Look it up and check it out.

What helps you deal with the prospect of illness, pain, and disability? Do the experiences of others bolster the belief that you, too, can live fully when reality doesn't go your way?

Calling

*Before I can tell my life what I want to do with it,
I must listen to my life telling me who I am.*
Parker Palmer

As our lives unfold, so do our options for making a contribution. Those options evolve with increased understanding of our strengths and passions. For many, midlife provides the impetus to serve in new ways that better conform to our self-awareness and sense of purpose.

Exactly Where We Need to Be

The winter of 1995-96 was the snowiest on record. I was far from home and family in Wisconsin, spending several months on a work project in New Hampshire. My career was stalled, and the assignment was intended to break it loose. With added drama, my employer (the federal government) was poised on the brink of shutdown over budget gridlock between the President and Congress. Furlough was imminent.

One Saturday morning during that time, I took a long drive by myself. Though feeling lonely and adrift, I savored the vision of New England at Christmas, with a candle and a wreath in every window. Along Main Street in another picture-perfect town, the sign for a small bookstore caught my eye. Within minutes I was scanning the shelves over a cup of hot cider.

An hour or so later, *Daily Meditations for Practicing the Course*, by Karen Casey, left the bookstore with me. It is now battered and taped after many years as a faithful companion. The meditation for New Year's Day remains my all-time favorite. I turn to it whenever I feel lonely and adrift, wondering what to do with my life.

"We are exactly where we need to be right now.

"It's good to be reminded that we are where we need to be, particularly if we're prone to think we are missing out on some opportunity or fearful that we aren't making significant progress in our careers or other areas. When we doubt that we're doing enough in any regard, this principle helps us quiet down and ready ourselves to peacefully do the next thing. It will always surface.

"It's comforting to realize there are no accidents, no coincidences happening in our lives. What we need to experience, to learn, to teach in order to complete our journey home will spring forth when the timing is perfect. We'll never have to search in vain for our next assignment. It will capture our attention.

"There are no mistakes in what comes my way today. How I respond depends on who I ask to help me see the circumstances."

I love the reminder that I can grow and serve in any setting. I appreciate the consolation that a wise and compassionate higher power walks at my side. A lifetime of experience confirms that those sentiments are not just the outgrowth of wishful fantasy but a profound reality to be accepted and embraced.

Where do you turn for inspiration in tough times? Do you find it comforting to believe there are no coincidences and no mistakes as our lives play out?

Lessons My Father Taught Me

It was 7:00 on a Thursday morning. Mother crawled into my bed, wrapped her arms around me, and whispered, "Honey, Daddy died during the night." I stayed home from school that day while she called family, made funeral arrangements, and planned the trip to bury my father in his home town two states away. It was a blur. I was stunned beyond pain. I was twelve years old, in seventh grade. Children my age didn't lose their parents. It couldn't be true.

My father was only 60 years old. He died of a sudden and catastrophic heart attack. He had retired just a few months earlier from a long career with General Motors. For as long as I could remember, he had hated going to work. Though he was a gifted engineer with many inventions and patents to his name, he did not march to the corporate drummer. As a profound introvert, he resisted the new design-team environment and refused to play office politics. He burned with resentment over the promotion of younger recruits. We crossed days off the family calendar, counting down to retirement day. We would take a long road trip across the country. He would spend more time in his woodworking shop. Maybe his quick temper would settle down. Life would be so much better when the time finally came.

I was young, and my memories are fuzzy. Nevertheless the lessons from that early experience have influenced my choices for a lifetime. I learned, first, the tragic cost of sticking with a situation that you hate. I changed fields several times before finding work that fit me well, and I am so glad that I did. The second lesson was not to put off until later what you can do today. I have made it a priority to build adventure and beauty into everyday life, and never to assume that a golden opportunity will last forever.

A third lesson, which evolved only with time, was that you don't have to leave a difficult environment to be happy. I have learned to deal with tough situations by improving my outlook, even when moving on was not an immediate option. It took more than three years to find a new position in the middle of my career. Though tempted by the boredom of repetition in the work I was doing at the time, I refreshed my commitment each year by volunteering for a special project or role.

Do you dislike your job? Are you putting off happiness until after you retire? What can you do today to make things better?

Mother Taught Me, Too

I learned some critical lessons about work and retirement when my father died at an early age. My mother also died young, at the age of 59, in the throes of job stress. Widowed twenty years earlier, she had found herself in the breadwinner role with little preparation or societal support. With marketable secretarial skills she found work quickly enough, but the pay was poor and did not include retirement benefits.

She was able to pay the mortgage and put food on the table but could not build the nest egg she needed to retire. She kept working through multiple phases of cancer treatment because her job offered minimal sick leave benefits and she could not resign without losing health insurance coverage.

I had seen the collision coming for several years. My mother dreaded going to work and was increasingly stressed by tight deadlines and poor staffing. She supervised employees whose performance was weak and conduct was worse. She expressed the dilemma: "I can't stand this job, but can't afford to retire." It felt afterward as if early death was her only escape.

I learned from growing up with my mother that financial security was an ideal, even if it seemed at the time an unattainable goal. I learned that the contract of lifelong support implicit in marriage could be broken in a heartbeat. I learned that gender bias in the workplace meant lower pay, less promotion potential, and fewer benefits for women than for men. I also learned that working in a job that felt like a trap could destroy the will to survive.

As I look back over a lifetime of rewarding work, I give thanks for opportunities unavailable to my mother, beginning with a college education and continuing with the rising tide of workplace equality. I am also grateful for a career that included financial security; its generous benefits allowed me to retire while healthy and strong. My mother's example helped me make work satisfaction, financial security, and retirement savings a priority. I also learned to approach the inevitable tough times with a constructive attitude, improving conditions where I could and accepting those that I could not change.

What lessons have you learned about work and retirement from your family's experience? How do those lessons affect the choices you make today?

Retirement: "Surprise!"

A few months ago, I celebrated the fifth anniversary of retirement from the U. S. Forest Service. Everyone notes that retirees wear such an unflinching smile, look so relaxed, and seem so healthy. All of the above are true for me, but the process of getting here has not been simple. Retirement was a milestone that marked endings and signaled beginnings for which I was only vaguely prepared. Five years offers a helpful perspective for reflecting on both the dream and the reality of stepping into the unknown. Looking back, I see a recurring theme: "Surprise!"

I am surprised with the ease of living well on less income. The ends are meeting, we are doing the things we enjoy, and we don't feel deprived.

I am surprised by the effort needed to start a business. I had planned to develop a life coaching practice after I retired. I wanted to help people, and assumed the need for extra income. So, after completing coach training I moved on to marketing. I took classes and read books; joined business organizations; developed a website and Facebook page; placed ads, and wrote a blog.

I built it, but it was hard for them to come. I barely opened the door. Without a financial motive, my urge to fill the calendar with appointments was lukewarm. Rather than connecting with potential clients, I often dropped the ball. I appreciate the clients who found me even though I was, to some degree, hiding from them.

I am, finally, surprised by the joy of volunteering. When business started slowly I found other ways to get involved. I started a Back of the Pack group in our running club. Shortly thereafter, the club decided to offer Jeff Galloway's run-walk-run marathon training program. They needed a program director, and I raised my hand.

Five years into retirement, a small life coaching practice fits into the larger picture of work I do for free. In both roles I can channel my passion for supporting others who want to transform their lives. The running club also fulfills my desires for friendship and belonging. With the discovery that we don't need more money, I have the luxury of donating my time and talent to this rewarding cause.

How do you envision retirement? What do you look forward to most after handing in the office key? How might you adapt if the first try doesn't turn out the way you expect it to?

Looking Forward, Looking Back

I was taking a class that required each of us to write our own eulogy. I had gone through this exercise before, and each time it was a different experience. My sense of life purpose and vision of success have evolved as I age. Each time, I focus on fewer points. Each time, the description of how I want to see myself at life's end is a little simpler.

I can now boil it down to one phrase: "I want to be truly helpful." What does that mean? Given my combination of temperament and experience, it probably does not mean that I can fix your car, host a large party, or transform clay and rocks into beautiful landscaping. Given the strengths with which I was born and the opportunities that followed, I am most helpful in less tangible ways. With that in mind, at the end of my life I want the following statements about me to be true:

She listened with understanding, accepted with openness, and appreciated the unique value of every person she encountered.

She supported others in aspiring to important personal goals and achieving them.

She walked the talk, living a life committed to learning and growth.

She shared the journey with compassion and insight.

She facilitated community, encouraging others to connect with common purpose.

I want to be truly helpful. I want to make a difference in the lives I touch. I want the world to be richer in kindness, patience, and humor for my being here. I want this vision to guide the choices I make today. And tomorrow. And the next day.

What lifetime contributions are most important to you? Do they resonate with your deepest values or do they still lean heavily on the expectations of others?

Can't Stop Talking

My supervisor asked, "So, tell me again: What do we do while we sleep?" We were wrestling with a complicated management decision fraught with drawbacks and risks. I had suggested that we "sleep on it." Bernie is an extrovert. I am an introvert. We have contrasting approaches to problem solving. He *talks* it through, while I *think* it through. This difference is just one way in which introverts and extroverts can misunderstand and judge one another.

I recently read *Quiet: The Power of Introverts in a World that Can't Stop Talking*. Author Susan Cain argues that U.S. culture is the most extroverted in the world. We collectively value those who think on their feet, decide quickly, prosper on teams, produce well in cubicles, and party hearty until the wee hours. Americans question the competence of those who pause before they speak, deliberate over decisions, want (and close) office doors, and go back to their rooms alone after a long day of meetings on the job.

Cain's book bridges a gap in understanding between people with different patterns: parents, teachers, and children; supervisors, employees, and coworkers. In a predominantly extroverted culture, extra effort is needed to understand and make room for the introverts in our midst. The following key points can enhance the process.

Extroverts restore energy by socializing; introverts by spending time alone.

Introverts respond poorly to noisy crowds, fast-paced presentations, bright lights, urgent deadlines, and other forms of intense stimulation.

Introversion arises within the brain and its chemistry. Some people are addicted while others are allergic to the adrenaline rush.

In the US, extroverts are encouraged to exhibit their natural traits. Introverts are counseled to exhibit behaviors that fit better into the dominant culture.

I find it helpful to understand the biological and cultural elements of my experience and that of other introverts. That understanding helps me navigate societal expectations without losing track of my own needs.

Are you more of an introvert or an extrovert? What about your spouse, children, boss? How do you blend your needs with those of others who flourish in a different way?

Find Your Strong

Yes, I am borrowing the phrase. Yes, you might have seen it elsewhere. Last year Saucony, the running shoe company, sponsored the "Find Your Strong Project." Customers were invited to submit quotes, videos, and other media that reinforced that message.

Credit duly given, I love the phrase. It bucks the cultural tide. News media fixate on human frailty, and my inner voice chides me when I fail. The to-do list enumerates the not-yet-done. I love being reminded to look, instead, for the strong. To celebrate how far I have come. To indulge the satisfaction of items crossed off the list.

Management guru Peter Drucker counsels leaders to get better results by focusing on employees' strengths, not their weaknesses. Psychologist Martin Seligman finds that those who know what they do best and exploit it achieve the most. Author Mihaly Csikszentmihalyi describes supreme happiness, or "flow," as engaging a challenging task that is perfectly matched to our skills. I was, on the other hand, raised in an era and by a culture in which the virtue of humility was exalted and pride derided as a deadly sin. It is hard for me to acknowledge and celebrate the things I do best.

I took a class in which we were assigned to ask loved ones to list our greatest strengths. (Was that ever hard to do!) I was astounded at the impact of their response. When I collected the qualities that those five people chose to notice, I felt a surge of inner power. I wanted to live up to their vision of me at my best.

A week later, after the initial shock of high-dose affirmation, I decided to return the favor. I wrote an email to each person, listing the strengths I saw. Their responses showed how much the experience meant to them as well.

Drucker is right. Seligman is right. Csikszentmihalyi is right. If we acknowledge and fully embrace our strengths, we can be more effective. If we obsess over our weaknesses, we might slow down and grind to a halt.

When have you been moved by a compliment on your character, talent, or strength? When have you taken the time to let someone else know what you appreciate about them?

Now You Can Stop

It was August 5, 1984 in the Los Angeles Coliseum. Her mother hugged her and whispered; "Now you can stop." Friends and supporters echoed the theme. "You've made your mark on history, now you can move on." Joan Benoit had won the first-ever women's Olympic marathon. Now she could settle down. Relax. Rest on her laurels. Get a life.

Joan herself saw it differently. Not one to dwell on past victories, she looked forward to more competition and continued to reach for the next level of excellence. Yes, she married Scott Samuelson. She birthed a daughter Abby and son Anders. She became active in supporting local environmental causes. But she also kept running, setting a string of world, American, and course records at the marathon distance.

When Joan turned 50, she focused her intent gaze on a new set of goals. She reconnected with winning the New York City and Chicago marathons in her youth by finishing in record time twenty-five years later. She delivered another strong Boston Marathon after winning in 1979 and 1983. She became the first woman to run marathons in under three hours in each of five decades. After having won the 1984 Olympic Marathon Trials, she wanted to qualify again, for the 2008 Trials, and missed by less than two minutes at the age of 51.

Joan Benoit Samuelson has finished every race she ever started. She still trains 85 miles a week in her 50s. She sets a goal, then while the medal still dangles from her neck, looks forward to the next one. She is not just out there, enjoying the admiration of her fans. She trains hard and puts forth her best effort. Every time.

Known by friends and fans alike as "Joanie," Samuelson stands as an icon of women's progress in athletics. At only 5'2", she is a giant in the world of running. Her example not only inspires because of her pinnacle successes but also because of her persistence over the decades. She has not only pursued personal goals over the years, but is well known for mentoring and motivating younger women to change their lives through running.

There is No Finish Line. What a perfect title for the documentary about Joanie's contribution as an individual athlete and as an ambassador for women in sport. I draw strength from her example to continue looking forward, with an eye to making the most of every day.

What goals do you want so much that they pull you into a life fully lived?
Which heroes embody the life you want as you move through the decades?

Faith in the Fog

Sweat. Nausea. A racing heart. Check, check, check. All the signs of terror, present and accounted for. Hundreds of taillights flickered in and out of view as we raced headlong into darkness. I wanted more than anything to slow down, to stop, to get off the road and breathe. But that was not an option.

Fear is still embedded in the memory from thirty years ago; the emotion is as clear as that night was not. Exhausted by a transatlantic flight, I had merged mindlessly onto the freeway out of LA International, then realized too late that coastal fog had rendered visibility near zero. Other drivers didn't notice; they were still going 70 miles per hour. I couldn't slow down, pull over, or stop without risking a rear-end crash.

I recently had a similar but gentler experience at home. When I got up that morning and glanced out the window for a view of city lights, the darkness was startling. It took a moment to recognize the fog of winter inversion. That time, I needed only retreat to the living room for the consolation of a warm fireplace until the fog lifted.

I struggle with fog at any speed. My desire for direction demands a clear view of the road ahead. My craving for certainty insists on orienting itself to the landscape. But we do not always get what we want. Fog, whether literal or metaphorical, is intrinsic to life. The questions hang in midair unanswered: Where am I? Where am I going? How do I get there?

I make plans. In fact, I make fantastic plans. I work out the details, generate what-if scenarios, and develop alternatives B, C, and D. I do my best to penetrate and prepare for the fog of possibilities that lie ahead. Yet, I am often surprised. I miss my flight. The projector breaks. I catch the flu. My business fails. What next?

It takes a stout spirit and firm resolve to wake and rise on foggy days. It takes even more to go outside and accelerate to freeway speed. Driving in the fog calls for caution. It calls for mindful attention to detail and intuitive response to changing conditions. It also calls for faith: the faith that other drivers will maintain an even speed and direction without dramatically slowing, veering off the road, or stopping without warning.

As I sat in the living room watching the sun break through, I reflected on the lesson of the day. It takes a stout spirit and firm resolve to wake and rise on any day, as every day has its large share of the unknown and unknowable. As I emerge from the safe cocoon of knowing where I am, I enter the hazy reality of where I am going. I trust in the strength, resolve, and intuitive wisdom to adjust, whatever appears.

How do the unknown and the unknowable affect your life? Can you proceed with faith? Where do you place your trust?

Easter, Sixto, and the Four Seasons

On a recent trip to Las Vegas, we enjoyed the popular musical, Jersey Boys. A few days later, we watched the Academy Award-winning documentary film, Searching for Sugarman. Then, during Easter week with its complex observance of joy and sorrow, I found myself comparing that ancient story with the other two, more recent ones.

Jersey Boys begins in a humble, blue-collar neighborhood in New Jersey. Its main characters have a rough start through drugs to jail, but over the course of 90 minutes they rise to stardom as Frankie Valli and the Four Seasons. Their upbeat songs still trigger an enthusiastic, toe-tapping response from Boomers who knew them when: *Sherry, Walk Like a Man, Big Girls Don't Cry*. Valli suffered many painful setbacks, including divorce and the loss of a daughter; but in the end, his story has success written all over it.

Sugarman begins in a humble, blue-collar neighborhood in Detroit. Its main character once played at a waterfront bar called The Sewer. Sixto Rodriguez cut two records, sold a few, and disappeared. Meanwhile his music made its way to South Africa and, unbeknownst to him, became a hit. The compelling tones of *Sugarman, I Wonder, and Crucify Your Mind* energized the movement to overturn apartheid and reinvent South African society. Forty years later, Rodriguez learned of his success and met his fans halfway around the world. He still lives a simple blue-collar life in Detroit, unchanged by late-breaking fame.

The Easter story begins in a humble inn-side stable in Bethlehem. It concerns a mysterious character who appears in public to teach key lessons, then retreats from center stage. The fans go crazy on Palm Sunday, and treat him like a rock star. His friends betray and abandon him on Holy Thursday. He is executed as a political criminal on Good Friday. His followers are consumed by grief, go to the grave, and find that he has risen from the dead. Two thousand years later, his powerful influence inspires and transforms lives around the world.

We don't always know when or how we are making a difference. I find that both unsettling and reassuring. We all have the same opportunity to wake up, give thanks for the day, and do our best. We can trust the rest of the story to unfold as it will.

What success stories do you find most inspiring? Where do you find wisdom and hope about the meaning and purpose of your life?

Morning Prayers

The little girl grew up taking long, silent, barefoot walks with her mother, wiggling her toes in the red New Mexico sand. The young woman entered a convent and dedicated her life to Christ. The mature woman traveled the world, inspiring thousands of listeners by braiding together strands from her Native American and Roman Catholic roots.

Sister José Hobday first enriched my life a few years ago through her first book, *Simple Living*. The journey continues with a second volume, *Stories of Awe and Abundance*. I am reflecting here on a chapter about the three elements of her childhood's Native American morning prayers. They welcome the day. They offer the self into service. They engage the Mystery behind all-that-there-is.

How often do I stop to celebrate the day ahead? I wake reluctantly, often retreating for a few more cycles of dreaming. After I roll out of bed, it is all about urgency: make coffee and check the calendar, the email, the to-do list, the weather report, the news. Before I know, day is done and I am frustrated by wondering where it went.

How often do I consciously dedicate myself to living the life I intend? I have many ideals. I want to be patient and generous, productive and creative, mindful and at peace. Nevertheless, my daily life is cluttered with false starts and setbacks. I get caught up in the ego's needs. I lose focus and waste time. I resist reality and rant about the way things should be.

How often do I transcend time and engage the Timeless? I am so enmeshed in plans and projects, cravings, conflicts, and control that I lose track of the larger perspective. When I do, the urgency fades and my appetites rest. I center on the spirit and find a better way.

As I reflect on a Native American version of morning prayers, I recall three favorite Christian prayers with similar themes. "This is the day the Lord has made, let us rejoice and be glad." "O Lord, make me an instrument of your peace." "Come Holy Spirit, fill the hearts of your faithful; kindle in us the fire of your love."

I have written those three prayers on a card for the table next to my morning chair. I look forward to starting the days ahead with the wisdom of Sister José.

How do you point yourself in the right direction each morning? Would you like to try something new?

When I Grow Up

His career plan was a dichotomous key, working back from the goal to build the steps that would take him there. My career plan was a rose in bud. It burst with potential, each petal hidden within until the next layer unfurled. He and I shared the stage in speaking to an assembly of younger employees. Twenty years later, one of them thanked me for helping her to embrace the fuzzy goals she had at the time and to trust in flow for the rest.

My experience with career has interwoven threads of strategy and surprise. Like my friend, I started out with a clear goal, took the prescribed steps, and landed precisely on target. Before long I saw that the job of my dreams didn't fit that well after all.

After leaving that field and embarking on another plan, I hit one wall after another. Then one day my car broke down far from home, and that one thing led to another beginning. A small-town job opening provided the unlikely entry to a rewarding long-term career.

Several years later, I set my sights on promotion but was discouraged by a series of fruitless job applications. I had come close to giving up when a chance encounter turned the tide.

When at last it came time to retire, I trained for a new profession and took the first unsteady steps toward starting my own business. While struggling to achieve the goal I had set, I began to volunteer. In the process, I have found work that I love enhanced by the freedom from marketing and business management.

These days I find myself in many conversations about work. My son and daughter-in-law are navigating the early stages of their careers. My friends in midlife face questions about changing employers, taking on more responsibility, or going into business for themselves. My peers wonder how to make the best use of their time and talents in retirement.

Though the details differ, the challenges we face at different times in our lives echo the childhood question, "What do you want to be when you grow up?" And though the details change, the journey through stages of work remains a creative blend of purposeful planning, disciplined preparation, sustained hard effort, and trust in the unknown.

What is your experience? Has your career turned out as planned, or has the magic of serendipity played a role? How would you encourage someone who feels stuck and wants to break loose?

Labyrinth in Life

A year ago, I announced that this would be my last season as a marathon training program director. After four years of commitment to this demanding and rewarding volunteer effort, I was ready to invest my retirement energy in something else. As the season draws to a close with next week's Missoula Marathon, I am still not sure what that "something else" might be.

Some days, I get all tied up in knots about it. Should I shift my emphasis to writing? Play and travel more? Offer to serve on nonprofit boards? Take up drumming? Recharge the life-coaching practice I have allowed to languish? With only a couple of years left in my seventh decade, the feeling of urgency is growing. The clock is ticking, and I want to get it right.

So, what is "getting it right," anyway? A few weeks ago, I visited the Red Sun Labyrinth in Victor, Montana. The first time I saw it, I envisioned a maze: Rats bouncing off dead ends in the search for cheese. Frustration. Claustrophobia. Trying, failing, and trying again. I did not know at the time that a labyrinth is a whole different kind of puzzle than a maze. It is a spiritual journey, not an intelligence test.

At Red Sun, the labyrinth is a lovely pattern etched in stones, surrounded by native landscaping. It looks up to snow-capped mountains and down to pastures dotted with horses and cows. I enter through a gap in the circle and follow the path. Back and forth, around, in and out, around again. Eventually, I reach the center. The path, though complex, is trustworthy. It requires no learning. It is not frustrating. It leads to the center; then, in reverse, it leads safely and surely to the world beyond.

My life sometimes feels like a maze. I set goals and miss them; experiment and fail; fall and get up. In truth, however, for nearly 70 years it has felt more like a labyrinth than not. Though the path has twisted and turned, I have always, in retrospect, appreciated the direction it took. Though I may not have seen the goal until I got there, and though it may not have looked like the end I had in mind, it has always been better than what I thought I wanted.

I have found that life, like a labyrinth, can be trusted. I don't have to figure it all out. I don't have to take control. I need only open my heart and confidently follow the spirit where it leads. I am curious and excited to see where it leads me next.

How do you experience the decisions that construct a path through your life? Are you frustrated by dead ends, or confident that a wise inner guide leads safely to the unknown future?

Connection

Peace of mind comes from not wanting to change others.
Gerald Jampolsky

Even the introverts among us are remarkably connected with others: family, friends, coworkers, business contacts, service providers, celebrities. We interact in a variety of roles and settings. Each encounter is an opportunity to develop an open mind, a generous and helpful heart, a grateful and forgiving soul.

Sparks and Smooth Edges

My generation is engaged in mass exodus from the world of work into the promised land of retirement. The journey is filled with joys and challenges. We enjoy the freedom to wake up when we are ready. We like to choose our own priorities, which often lead to more play and less drudgery. One friend describes her journey as "more being, less doing."

While the joy of more freedom is one recurring theme; another, on the challenge side of the ledger, is at least as common. We are sharing more time and space with life partners after decades of coming and going from separate worlds. That transition can have rough edges.

Like rocks and minerals, we develop an irregular shape over the course of our lives. Our psyches harden with habit and we identify deeply with our preferences and opinions, values and schedules. Early to rise or late to bed, many projects or few, more play or more work, social life vs. solitude, travel or not and (if so) where and for how long? Some couples sail through the transition to these new choices on a wave of unconditional love and mutual consideration. I don't know those couples. The rest of us have to deal with rough edges.

Like other inner demons we encounter on life's adventure, rough edges provide us with a choice. We can insist and resist. Rough edges embodied in flint and steel generate sparks, heat, and fire. Most fires are small and go out on their own; others expand and overwhelm the commitment of years. Divorce is an unsettling trend among the recently retired.

Rough edges can also be seen as smooth stones waiting for release. As we rub against one another's hard edges and sharp points, we can choose to re-frame our absolutes in relative terms. Maybe there is space in this household for more than one opinion or more than one approach to scheduling the day. Perhaps we can learn to enjoy something we never tried before. Maybe it is OK for our partners to pursue separate interests while we pursue ours, comparing notes at the end of the day.

Rough edges do not wait for retirement to emerge, and they are not unique to couples. We rub against differences with others all the time: at home, at work, in the neighborhood, on the highway. We are faced hour-to-hour with a choice between insisting on our way, accommodating the demands of another, or seeking a solution that works for us both.

Where in your life do the rough edges rub? How do you work with the heat and light that result?

Gratitude Alert

It is always dark and lonely in Missoula at 4:30 on a winter morning, but this particular morning it was even more so. We were under a blizzard alert. Snow had been falling heavily all night on an icy layer of freezing rain. Winds had whipped up drifts. Snowplows had not yet reached our neighborhood. Lyle was taking a 5:30 flight from the airport across town. It was hard getting out of the driveway, but backing downhill gave me momentum to get onto the street. Coming back was a different story.

It is especially dark and lonely in Missoula at 4:30 am in a blizzard. It is even more so when you are stuck in a snowdrift, half-in-half-out of the driveway and a snowplow roars by within inches of your bumper. It is daunting to dig out with a small shovel and a bad back after that plow has pushed up a berm of additional snow to pen you in. I was near tears, but tears in a blizzard don't do much good, so I started to dig. The digging didn't last long.

A small pickup truck pulled up on the dark, lonely street and the two guys inside asked if I needed help. Yes! They jumped out and with youthful vigor cleared the snow in minutes. They made sure I got up the driveway and into the garage. They handed back my shovel and, with it, my newspaper.

Overflowing with gratitude, I sent a message to the newspaper's circulation department. I posted a thank-you on Facebook (it was re-posted and triggered nearly 800 "Likes"). I shared my experience with the neighborhood mailing list. I wrote a thank-you note and included a tip. This is not the first time I have been touched by the kindness of strangers, but again it comes with surprise. Self-sufficiency and urgency are cultural norms that inhibit the helping hand. Customers down the street may well have been grumbling because their papers were later than usual that day; little did they know (and would they have cared about?) the reason why.

The merging of need and response did not stop there. A week has passed since two men in a small pickup truck made mine a better day in the blizzard at 4:30 am. Every morning since, they have come up the driveway and delivered my paper to the porch instead of leaving it by the mailbox as usual. We are still strangers, but we are connected by a bond of giving and receiving, generosity and gratitude.

What lessons have you learned from giving and receiving unexpected acts of kindness? What goes through your mind when you are in a hurry and someone else's need comes into view?

Reconnecting with Love

When I was in college, November was the hardest month. Milwaukee with its damp, cold winds blowing off Lake Michigan penetrated not only my clothing but my spirit. I struggled to maintain a veneer of happiness and the pretense of inner peace.

As October drew to a close this year, I heard an echo of those earlier times. Instead of external factors like weather, however, I became acutely aware of gaps in connection with relationships that I treasure. I wondered what was happening and what to do about it. On the one hand, I wanted to call or to visit, to write a long email or a letter. On the other hand, I considered the possibility that our lives had drifted apart. Perhaps it was time to let go.

We hear about the importance of social connection for health and longevity. We also see how those connections are challenged over time. The family into which I was born is, for the most part, gone. The community of co-workers and the rituals of daily teamwork have faded since I retired. The role of our only son in our daily lives has changed since he grew up, left home, and married. Friends are pulled in many directions and the only constant thread, woven through it all, is change.

It is November 1. The sun rose late this morning, casting a weak light on fog in the valley. My November neurosis anticipated a gray and rainy day. Then I got up off the chair and looked out the window to the east. There on the horizon were puffy white clouds tinged with peach and salmon and gold. Sunlight was creeping across the hillsides. It was a bright new day and a hopeful harbinger of the month ahead.

I exchanged long emails with a distant friend, lined up lunch with another, and a hike with someone else. I scheduled a movie with my husband and wrote a letter to his parents. I am looking for a treat to send our son and his bride to help them ride out this tough semester of graduate school.

When I started writing today, I wobbled at the top of a slippery slope. I felt the threat of a cold and gray early winter day and a void of connection with family and friends. I was on my way down. Then something changed. A glimmer of light shone on the horizon and spread to my brain. I remembered to reach out. My loved ones reached back.

Are you out of touch with someone you love? What might you do today to re-tie the cord that joins you?

Flu Season

The proliferation of insistent messages finally reached me. On the way home yesterday, I stopped at Walgreens, pulled out my new Medicare card, and got a flu shot. The last time I had the flu, I was in college and burning the candle at both ends. Since then, my immune system has served me well. What makes it different this year? Is it just the relevance of advice to seniors over 65? No, it is something else.

I recently read that vaccination is not only an act of individual self-care, but a communal one as well. The more of us who develop resistance to infection, the fewer infected people are spreading viral joy. That made sense to me, and played a role in baring my arm to the needle.

Upon reflection, I discovered that vaccination as a metaphor can be broadly applied. Not only does my own personal virus threaten the larger community, but so does my own personal state of mind. Who else suffers when I allow pessimism to fester? Who else is infected when I succumb to irrational fear? Who else catches the bug when I harbor resentment? I can make the case that my feelings are a personal problem and that I alone suffer the consequences. On the other hand, I also acknowledge the risk of contagion.

As I anticipate the close quarters of holiday air travel, I take comfort from the protection a flu shot provides for me and for others. As I look forward to the close emotional quarters of holiday gatherings, I also want to immunize myself from the contagious negative outlooks that can spread so quickly around a room.

It is easy to infuse social conversation with bad news. Pain and misery are sometimes the cheapest tickets to a party. When tempted to add my voice to a gloomy mix, I want to ask, myself first, "at what price?" When I catch the bug of complaining and pass it along, my own mood dives and I bring others along on my way down. In contrast, I can offer an upbeat story. A compliment. An "I love you." A "thank you." What a difference it could make!

In immunizing myself from the emotional risks of negative conversation, I am carrying a small book of meditations to refresh my view. I am journaling gratitude, seeking out good news in the world, in my life, and around the family table. I am starting some conversations by asking, "What is going well for you?"

How do you build immunity toward negative thoughts and feelings? How do you protect the others with whom you rub shoulders and share airtime?

Family Ties, Bows, and Knots

My husband comes from a large family. As an only child whose parents have been gone a long time, I respond to his family ties on several emotional levels.

On the deepest and most basic level, I am grateful. We were married the year my mother died. "Going home" to spend Christmas with his family in Wisconsin that year was a first big step toward filling the void. The new family ties were a gift, tied with a bow. I have spent Thanksgiving or Christmas there for more than 30 years, and the scene of a large family gathering scheduled for halftime has become my own beloved vision of a holiday meal. I give thanks for the stability of repetition and take comfort from the persistence of traditions over time.

On another level, I am conflicted. Marriage is a coming together of differences. Those differences shine brightly when reflected in the faces of extended family. They echo and reverberate in the voice of longstanding rituals. There is a right way to peel potatoes, dice cabbage, frost cookies. Mom's pumpkin pie will always be the best.

Traditions solidify family bonds; they enhance the sense of belonging among those with whom longstanding habits are shared. Traditions can also have unintended results. However trivial they seem, they can foster a sense of separation. Contrasting traditions and bursts of creativity are viewed with discomfort. "Salsa and chips?" "Sweet potatoes without marshmallows? Brussels sprouts?" A potluck meal turns into an identity check: Are you one of us, or one of them? Family ties can bind, and tie us in knots.

Now we, too, are family-in-law. I want to learn from the experiences I have shared. I want Jennie to feel welcome because we honor her family history and her unique individuality. I want to develop new traditions and to include her in their design. It's too early to know how it will work; we haven't yet been blessed with a holiday together. My intentions are good, but we all know where that pavement can lead.

How do your families weave together the diverse strands of tradition? Are your family ties loose enough to wrap a larger package in an assortment of bows?

Peas and Butter, Mother and Me

Mother's Day always carries a bittersweet taste for the daughter in me. The sweet comes with gratitude for the woman who gave me life; the bitterness, with re-living her loss to aggressive cancer over 30 years ago. I typically let the day come and go gently, without much fanfare. This year, however, I am moved to reflect on two memorable excerpts from our mother-daughter experience.

Let's begin with peas. I grew up in Indiana in the 1950s, when much of our food came in cans. I hated canned peas. I made quite a fuss about it, and quite an impression on my mother. Then I discovered frozen peas, and have loved them ever since. Until she died, however, my mother "knew" that I hated peas. No matter how I protested to the contrary, she made sure that they were never on our menu.

Butter has a different story. I moved to California in the late 1960s, where I lived with a weirdly wonderful mix of roommates. When Mother came to visit, we threw a potluck in her honor. Everyone sat, crowded and cross-legged on the floor, balancing plates on our knees. As the butter dish passed to my mother, it tipped and the stick rolled to the floor. After a brief pause, she picked up it up, restored it to the plate, took her share, and passed it along.

Ever since her passing, I still treasure the butter story and carry some lingering annoyance about peas. Between the two, they reveal two faces of motherhood. On the one hand, our mothers have known us from the beginning. Sometimes their memories don't make room for us to grow. Our mothers' memories of our immaturity can embarrass and hold us hostage. On the other hand, our mothers also grow and change. Even a traditional, proper, Midwestern mom can sit on the floor, get into the groove, and eat butter off the floor.

As parents and children, we are tempted to freeze one another in the past. We capture key memories, cast them in concrete, and believe that they tell it all. As parents and children we are perpetual works in progress: changing, growing, surprising, exploring, and pushing the edge. As parents and children we can serve not only as guardians of a shared past, but also as cheerleaders for an unlimited future.

As a daughter who lost her mother so long ago, it is easy for me to freeze her image in time. I am tempted to think I knew her, to believe my own stereotypes of what she thought and how she felt. Sometimes, however I delight in the glimpse of her picture through fresh eyes. She not only raised me to respect and follow the rules, but she also broke with tradition and exceeded the limits of her own upbringing, and not only when it came to butter.

How do you see your mother, daughter, or son? Does your love confine, or does it celebrate and expand the family picture to incorporate change?

Tree Casts a Shadow

A few months ago, I asked some friends: "I'm thinking of a tattoo…what do you suggest?" Two of them replied, *"The Giving Tree."* The phrase sounded familiar, and seemed to be a compliment, but I didn't dig any deeper at the time. Then, a few weeks ago, another friend proposed that I consider *The Giving Tree* as a metaphor to explore in developing my coaching practice. She reminded me of Shel Silverstein's picture book by that name. With a one-click online purchase, I found the book (and so much more).

The Giving Tree has generated substantial controversy on its way to becoming an American legend. As I suspected, the book has thousands of favorable reviews. Many people admire the selfless giving embodied in the tree whose long-term friendship with a boy carries him through decades of evolving needs. The tree feels some sadness at his failure to give back, but does not withhold her gifts or demand a balance of tit for tat. The book ends when the boy cuts down the tree to build a house, and sits reflectively on the stump that remains. For many readers, the story portrays the inspiring reality of maternal love, of divine love, of an unconditional love that gives without counting the cost.

Others, however, are furious at Silverstein for appearing to condone such behavior. They blame him for encouraging "enablers" whose generosity perpetuates the self-absorption of others. They point to a misguided generosity that has entrapped countless women in the service of families who take them for granted. They consider the tree a poor role model at best; a deluded and destructive neurotic at worst.

My encounter with the tree and her boy has triggered serious personal reflection. I do want to love. I want to serve. I aspire to a degree of generosity that stretches me to be less self-centered. My spiritual role models gave all; why shouldn't I consider that the ideal? But the "other side" has a point as well.

I have taken another look at giving past the point of depletion and the self-care that sustains our capacity to serve. I have searched in dark corners for gifts with attached strings that entangle the purity of our intent. In the process, I have learned that the blessings of giving are interwoven with the importance of asking and perhaps, on occasion, withholding a gift with generous intent.

Do you know "The Giving Tree?" What thoughts and feelings does she engender in you? How do you interpret her message for your own life?

How Can I Help?

"I am here only to be truly helpful." For the nearly three decades since I first read it in *A Course in Miracles*, that phrase has guided my sense of purpose. It is a simple statement and points to a simple "yes" in the moment of choice. Much of the time. Not now. Not that simple.

Along with millions of other Baby Boomers, we have embarked on a family journey into aging and changing roles. We are coming to terms with introducing a caregiver role with our parents and swapping it for the comforts of being cared for. They changed our diapers, helped us dress, and guided our faltering steps. It is our turn. I am not ready. Will I ever be?

What does it mean to be truly helpful in this picture? I remember sitting at the kitchen table as a child, hunched over a coloring book as my mother and her sister shared concerns about my grandmother: "We can't let her..." "We have to make her..." "She can't do that." Something about that conversation troubled me deeply. They were the children; she was the parent. How could they talk about her that way?

My own mother died young. She took me by surprise. Less than halfway across the bridge of denial, I realized she was gone. I was determined to learn from that painful experience and to do better the next time I was offered a chance. Lyle's mother is living a long life. She has spent more than 90 years raising a family, baking cookies and pies, hosting everyone on the holidays. She has faithfully sent birthday cards to three generations of offspring and, as they have married, to their spouses. That is changing. Her attention span, her energy, and her strength have diminished...slowly at first, now at a quickening pace.

The little girl in me still shrinks from switching roles. I recoil from the appearance of treating a parent as if she were a child. On the other hand, I fear using respect as an excuse for distance. The needs for help are real. They are not all pretty, and seldom easy. I remind myself that practical assistance need not carry patronizing overtones.

I need help, the kind of help that comes with prayer. I do not know what would be helpful. I do not know what is needed and whether I can provide it. But it is not about me. The passage from *A Course in Miracles* continues, "I do not need to worry about what to say or what to do, for He who sent me will direct me. I will be healed as I let Him teach me how to heal."

How have you dealt with your loved ones as minds and bodies fall short? How have you negotiated the learning curve to playing a different role?

Tripping Over Sweetie

"Why aren't you at work?" "I am at work." "Ohhh..." This succinct dialogue between Gwen and Scott took place a few months ago. He forgot, however briefly, that she had retired the day before and was at home working on her novel. This was the new normal, and he would get used to it eventually.

Variations on this scene play out hundreds of times a day as the newly retired show up unexpectedly in a strange and different place: their own home. In many families, one partner retires first, or serves as the home-maker, or develops a home-based business. That partner has gotten used to having their own time and space to spare. The other has been looking forward fondly to the ideal of a home-based life. After years of commuting and working in a cubicle or factory or classroom, the idea of home is warm and fuzzy with appeal.

The reality may produce a tangle of mismatched expectations, communication breakdowns, and even some resentment until new patterns form. Those who anticipate and prepare for the change may have an edge over those who don't, but very few couples make the transition without a bump or two.

How do I use my time? And in which rooms? When? How much and what kind of noise do you make? Do I clean up after myself? Do you? Do you sleep in? Do I hang out in PJs all morning? Do I close the door to work on a project? Do you feel rejected? Does my nap look lazy to you? Are you eating again? Surfing? Watching soaps? Why didn't you tell me where you were going? I was worried. Stop treating me like a child!

I thought we knew each another well after 30 years, but the dance of retirement required a whole new set of moves for Lyle and me. It felt awkward to negotiate trivia like newlyweds. In a sense, however, we were building a new version of wedded bliss. We still trip over each another five years later, but we do so much less often. We have woven together two very different patterns of sleeping and waking, working and playing, eating and exercising, coming and going, into a mostly harmonious whole. We schedule time together for a beer on the porch, concert in the park, or pizza downtown. We also respect the need for independence and time alone, especially now that we live full-time under a single roof.

Is sharing time and space a challenge for you? What new patterns have you tried for gracefully re-designing your relationship to fit the new pattern?

Thinking of You

Sending prayers. How can I help? I am so sorry. Best wishes. Phrases like these express our oh-so-inadequate desire to reach out, connect, and support one another in times of trial. I have had many occasions to use these phrases in recent months. In doing so, I have been reflecting on the vocabulary of loving connection and the meaning underlying the words. I have concluded that the phrase and reality that mean the most to me are, "thinking of you."

Our minds are always racing: things to do, reactions and judgments, plans and hopes, analysis and evaluation. It takes heartfelt effort to make space for thoughts that reach out to another in need. It takes another increment of effort to write the note, send the email, post the Facebook comment, or make the call that lets them know. When I recently shared some personal struggles in my weekly *Reflections*, the responses of readers and outreach from others made a powerful difference. They gave me the strength of sharing the burden and relying on the power of team effort.

The power comes not only from offers of practical help, welcome though they are. Yes, I need help with snow when Lyle is away; and I love you, neighbor, for plowing unasked. And thank you for watching to see that newspapers don't pile up. Yes, I could use a ride to the airport. Yes, the book you sent will feed my quest for perspective. Those are all wonderful gifts, but (and I risk a cliché) the thought behind the gift counts most.

It is easy to feel invisible and alone, especially during tough times. I am not the best company when depressed or anxious; absorbed in myself, I withdraw. Any gesture that strengthens the web of relatedness under these circumstances is precious. "Thinking of you" remembers and reminds me of events we have shared. "Thinking of you" knows the music I like. "Thinking of you" retrieves our past conversations and applies them to new challenges. "Thinking of you" may not know what to say or do but shows up anyway.

We all have different talents. I admire those who choose the perfect gift, deliver a pot of healthy home-made soup, or offer a healing massage. None of those is a talent of mine. But I can think of you. I can send you the note that tells you so. I can remember our conversation and send you a link to the video we discussed. I can call you for a coffee date and listen as well as talk. I pray for the grace to offer what I can when the need arises.

What thoughtful gestures from others stand out in your experience? What talents and gifts of thought and connection come most naturally when you reach out to someone else?

May I Take Control?

Midnight in Mumbai. Morning in Missoula. Atul had just asked if he could take control. He pointed me to the screen, and assured me, "If at any time you feel uncomfortable, hit the red X and the session will end."

Still, how would I know when I felt *that* uncomfortable? I had been uncomfortable, at best, since my anti-virus program shut down an hour earlier, unwilling to restart. I had run through half a dozen do-it-yourself options, and ended up clicking the "Support" button. Now I was handing over my computer, its function, its data, and my personal identity to a stranger halfway around the world. I was uncomfortable. Anxious. Borderline paranoid. But I didn't hit the red X. I needed help.

Darkening in Missoula. Dawning in Mumbai. He handed it back. We had gone through the day together, taking breaks for my lunch meeting and afternoon appointment. Each time I came back, he was there, cheerful, ready to pick up where we left off. While he worked, I followed the confident mouse-strokes that cleared problem files, scanned, uninstalled, reinstalled, dejunked, and tuned up.

He asked if I would like anything else. I declined, and thanked him for his patience and persistence during the day. "Good morning." "Good evening." I felt genuine warmth and connection after many hours of coming and going together by phone and live chat. Atul had transformed from scary stranger into valued partner in reversing my computer's very bad day.

Yes, I know even now that a bad experience could be lurking behind the good one. The computer worked fine last night, but will a secret bug come to life later? What about the personal info? Credit card numbers, passwords...the kinds of things we hold close. Somewhere along the way I had to decide whether to continue struggling with a problem I was unable to solve, or to relinquish control.

This experience repeats every day of our lives. We want so much to be autonomous, self-sufficient, in control; yet every day we hit our limitations. We need help. We let go of control. We trust doctors with our bodies, mechanics with our cars, bankers with our money. I am amazed at how heavily we depend and thrive on the goodwill of unknown others. We take precautions, but we cannot live a life that protects us from everything and everyone that could potentially harm us. My life was enriched by spending the day with Atul. I moved past initial frustration with his accent and the reality of outsourcing to form a bond that connected my need with his expertise. The world is a little smaller, a little friendlier, a little more diversely linked as a result.

What is your experience with the unknown and its hidden threats? How have you dealt with the decision to let go (or when to hit the red X and bail)?

Weaving on the Web

This morning, Facebook suggested I might want to connect with "Jim." The name struck a bell, and this person lives in the city where we met (if I have the right guy) over 50 years ago. Given his home town and the background I remember, we could feasibly have those two Facebook friends in common.

I may follow up with a message asking if he is indeed the "Jim" from my teens.

Some people consider a Facebook match like this one as spooky. Some see it as scary. I see it as miraculous. I see it as a metaphor for the metaphysical hypothesis that we are all, indeed, one.

Facebook is a place to explore our connectedness. I know these three people; do I also know the fourth? We went to the same high school. We love cats. We are inspired by the same wisdom literature. We run, paint, sing, or write. The breadth of topics on which we find kindred spirits seems to have no bounds.

Facebook is a place to build community. I risk the accusation of naiveté in making such a statement, knowing as I do that experts deride virtual relationships as unhealthy alternatives to the real thing. I do embrace the flesh-and-blood reality of living, working, and playing with others in real time. I also love connecting across vast expanses of uncommon ground with people I may never meet face-to-face.

I share the Facebook experience with fellow life coaches, writers, beer lovers, Forest Service retirees, and alumni of every school I attended. Last week, I "friended" two men in Australia who are starting a back-of-the-pack running group much like ours. This morning I reached out to a former boss and a former professor. And then there is "Jim."

Interacting on Facebook is, I admit, an addictive habit (along with checking email, the weather, the news, sports scores, inspirational passages-of-the-day, and Simon's new cat video on YouTube.) I know that I risk tipping the balance from enjoying to craving online treasure. I take that risk willingly.

The weaving together of past and present relationships, deep and shallow ones, frequent and occasional ones into a colorful whole enriches my life and expands my horizon to a truly global scale.

What is your experience with social media and other connections with people you may never meet in person? Do you see it as escaping or enhancing your face-to-face engagement with others in your life?

Energy

*The number of hours in a day is fixed, but the quantity
and quality of energy available to us is not.*
Jim Loehr & Tony Schwartz

How often do we lament the lack of time in our lives? I hear it every day, and say it myself on most: "I don't have time enough for that." Though I use it anyway, that disclaimer rings hollow for me. Though we all have the same twenty-four hours in a day, the amount we fit in and the satisfaction we feel seem to differ greatly. It makes sense that our limits relate more to energy than time. Time is unproductive when energy is below par. On reflection, I have discovered that energy grows when calling, connection, and adventure converge to motivate optimal use of the time I am given.

Renewable Energy

The pursuit of personal energy is a recurring theme on my life journey. I want more. I am not sure how to get it. I scour books and magazines for magic formulas. Energy is elusive. It requires adequate hydration, the right vitamins, and a good night's sleep. Too much coffee is worse than too little. Exercise helps, but can also hurt. The advice doesn't always work.

In *The Power of Full Engagement,* Jim Loehr and Tony Schwartz compile the elements of optimal energy into a simple but comprehensive whole. Drawing from the field of sports performance, they describe the universal training model of exertion followed by recovery. When building strength, endurance, or flexibility an athlete pushes the body slightly past its limits. For performance to improve, extra effort must alternate with cycles of rest. Fatigued muscles rebuild. Depleted cells replenish.

Mental, emotional, and spiritual performance also benefit from alternating between effort and recovery. We tend to run our daily lives on the traditional model of a marathon: sustained effort at a consistent pace for hours at a time. These authors prefer the metaphor of a sprint, with its burst of speed followed a slow jog; engagement and disengagement. Repeat. As business consultants, Loehr and Schwartz have discovered that the "corporate athletes" they work with perform best when concentrated efforts alternate with changes of scene and pace. They call the process "oscillation."

I have adopted the practice of oscillation and apply it to the energy cycles of everyday life. An hour of study and a walk on the treadmill. Writing and housework. A long run and a hot bath. Mowing the lawn and taking a nap. When I punctuate time with cycles like these, my energy is more likely to last all day.

How does your energy hold up when you work long hours without a break? Have you tried oscillating between effort and recovery? What have you found?

Flow and the Fourth of July

On July 4, 1776, the Second Continental Congress adopted the Declaration of Independence. That document affirmed certain inalienable rights, including the right to pursue happiness. We grew up with that phrase, but how often do we ask what it means? How often do we exercise that right in our daily lives?

Happiness, like energy, is an elusive target. We want it and the more of it the better. We think we will know it when we see it. When asked to describe it, we falter. The answer is often framed as an absence of suffering. We understand suffering.

Of the many books that address the topic of happiness, a perennial favorite of mine is *Flow*. Flow is a state of profound engagement in which time stops and we are captured by the richness and depth of the moment. Flow finds that sweet spot between boredom and anxiety in which the challenge we face equals our capacity to meet that challenge. Flow energizes action for its own sake, not as the means to a future goal.

Star athletes, champion chess players, accomplished musicians, and participants in extreme sports experience flow. So can we. Attention to the moment and its intrinsic value gives us a good start. Activities that exercise our skills at their highest level take us farther down the path. Improving those skills so that their limits increase and our delight expands in turn can generate even more potential for flow. Skills come in many forms: athletic, artistic, culinary, intellectual, interpersonal, organizational, and more. We are programmed to seek and to find joy wherever we grow.

Flow describes happiness as a high-energy mode of being, not as a static goal. Flow can be described; it can even be pursued; but only in the present moment, not sometime in the future.

What skills do you most enjoy using? How do you tap into the energy they produce? Exercise the rights upon which our nation was founded; go out and pursue some happiness.

Whitewater

The discussion of flow leads me through free association to the metaphor of whitewater, introduced by my friend Jane several years ago. In looking ahead to an extra-busy week, she wrote that she was perched on the bank of a fast-moving stream, preparing to jump in and hoping to stay afloat. We have often returned to that image over the years.

If the energy of flow arises with a perfect match between skill and challenge, whitewater pushes the limits and calls us to develop further. In whitewater, the current is powerful and the hydraulics complex. The movement is swift and our responses intuitive. Small errors of judgment can flip us and carry us on an even wilder ride.

Those who run whitewater well have developed skills in planning, presence, and recovery. They plan by studying the river in advance, running it repeatedly in their imaginations until the pattern of flow and response is engrained in their being. They employ presence in the midst of action. When in motion, they don't think things through and weigh the options; they don't worry about what will happen next. They are intensely present, focused on the demands of the millisecond. When upsets occur, and they always do, a master of the sport knows how to flip upright in an instant, recovering both balance and momentum.

In order to tap the energy of a fast-flowing life, we can emulate the skills of those who run rapids for fun. Look ahead, memorize the current. Design strategies for unexpected twists and turns. Rehearse. While in motion, silence the fearful mind. Attend to what is happening now, and trust in training and intuition for a skillful response. When the boat overturns, flip back up with a few deft strokes and go with the flow.

Are you busy? Check out the days ahead. Where are the holes, the eddies, and the rocks? Are you ready? Go for it. If not, find a portage around the hazards.

White Space

Several years ago, facing a chaotic and overcrowded schedule, I explored the metaphor of whitewater rapids. The metaphor resurfaced recently as I rode a surge of intensity around my volunteer commitments on Missoula Marathon weekend. A few days later, I reflected on the value of creating white space on a calendar that had filled to overflowing.

I felt the urge to do it all: the hike, the pub run, breakfast with one friend and lunch with another, the vendor booths, the seminar, two pizza parties, and more. I wanted to watch fireworks at the start and hug the last person when he crossed the finish line eight hours later. I am pleased to say that maturity and perspective eventually won out, and I found ways to pause and re-charge between major events.

Some of you probably wonder what I am fussing about. It's all good! Why not get up earlier, stay up later, and pack it all in? After all, you can catch up on sleep when everything settles down a few days later, right? Not for me, and not for the others of you whose copy of Susan Cain's *Quiet* is tattered and worn. Falling at the introverted end of the temperament scale, I feel not only fatigued and grouchy but physically ill when over-socialized and over-stimulated during times like these. For many years, I just felt guilty that I couldn't match the energy I saw in my peers. Then, as I learned more about the personality spectrum, I came to accept and honor my needs even when they differ from those of the mainstream.

I skipped some events and cut others short. I asked friends to fill behind me here and there. I drove to a shady park and read the paper. I had a beer with one friend instead of joining hundreds more at an event down the street. I went home for a midday nap. I skipped the starting line to be fresh for the last finisher of the day.

The results were gratifying. My levels of activity and social connection over marathon weekend exceeded my norm, yet I had a wonderful time. I emerged with a smile and the passion for more. That hasn't always been true. When I have allowed a sense of duty and unquestioned desire to make it all fit rule my decisions, I have burned out and bordered on resentful. Taking the initiative to open white spaces and use them for recovery worked so well, I think I will do it again.

Are you challenged by a congested calendar and back-to-back social events? Do you chide yourself for losing energy when others keep going? How might you see and do it a different way?

Frame It and Paint It

Like energy and happiness, time seems to come in short supply. It doesn't meet all the needs and wants that we ask of it. "So many books, so little time," is a magnet on our fridge. We have all heard variations on that theme.

I was once asked to bring a creative product to share during a teambuilding session. With no artistic or musical talents, I struggled with the assignment. Eventually I assembled a collage designed around the combination of activities in my life at the time. I described time as a canvas, the activities as a palette of colors from which to choose. That metaphor still works for me. I enjoy painting a picture on the canvas of time far more than fighting once again to fit everything onto the crowded pages of a day-planner.

Some blocks of time are a paint-by-number set. Many work days have that appearance. The shapes are in place, and little numbers correspond to the prescribed colors: budget meeting (15), conference call (33), and performance rating (07). As much as they frustrate freedom of expression, a quality paint-by-number project can be lovely. It represents a whole that builds a larger picture out of smaller parts. A busy work day can also be pretty.

Other days feel more like a coloring book. The lines are there, but we can choose any color we want to fill them in. Maybe we get the giant box of crayons and can choose burnt ochre, magenta, or peach as well as red, yellow, and blue. I think of the typical weekend as a coloring book with pictures in outline form. Errands to run, family events, and social occasions: The structure is there, but we have freedom to make it our own with shades and tones.

Then, at last, we confront the scary magic of a blank canvas! The family is at a soccer tournament or we have the day off when everyone else is at work or school. Or we retire and the size of the blank canvas expands. What to do? Pull out the paint-box and the imagination. Sketch a few lines to suggest a shape or two, then go for the color and the pattern and the image that arise from a vast reservoir of possibilities. Such a day can be as simple or as complex as you make it, and the definition of beautiful is left to you.

Time-as-art does not solve the problem of fitting too many tasks into a given day. It may, however, enrich the effort. If we see our day as a canvas, and strive to make each day beautiful in its own way, we may just have a burst of joy that would not otherwise appear.

What does the blank canvas of an empty calendar suggest to you? How will you fill it in with shapes, patterns, and colors?

Investing the Gift

Time management is an ongoing dilemma for me. While not a life-or-death issue, I have always wanted to make better use of the days, weeks, and months allotted to my life. The bookcase is jam-packed with time management titles. I have read them all. Each has its own value, but no single system works for me all the time. After I retired, the challenge ramped up with the lack of structure in my schedule and an increased range of enticing opportunities.

I can easily manage the day-to-day: tracking appointments, keeping a to-do list, setting and meeting deadlines for minor projects. It is much more difficult to handle longer time frames and larger-scale goals. How would I design the time to write a book? Start a business? Maintain long-term relationships and develop new ones? Grow in wisdom and grace? When those larger goals overwhelm me, I grind to a halt. I go to bed early and sleep late, putter, shop, nibble endlessly, and surf the web.

As the years of retirement accumulate, I still wrestle with patterns of escape and procrastination, but not as much as I used to. I have learned a lot by experimenting and have made some key discoveries. I do well with a mix of structured and unstructured time. I enjoy a balance of solitude and social contact. I thrive on a blend of learning and productivity, reading and writing. Morning is best for mental focus; early afternoon for socializing and exercise; evenings for paying bills, pulling weeds, cleaning house, or laundry.

I have also found that I flourish within broad and flexible structure. At the beginning of each month, I develop a few over-arching themes and brainstorm a list of activities under each. Each week, I move a few of those activities to the current to-do list. That approach keeps me moving in small steps toward large goals without becoming overwhelmed.

In truth, we never manage time. Time flows on its own, with or without us. We have the opportunity to see each day, month, and year as a gift and to learn from experience how to make the best of that gift. We often talk about spending time. I am replacing "spend" with "invest." I often spend both time and money poorly; it is gone, but where did it go? Investment requires that we value a resource and understand its potential to grow if we pay attention and make decisions thoughtfully.

How do the options of saving, spending, or investing time play out in your daily life?

Counting Sheep

When I consider energy, I think first about the body. My own energy seems to start there. Without adequate physical energy, other systems chug along slowly or stop altogether. The body needs many resources to function well; food, water, activity and sleep are foremost among them. I want to reflect here on the challenge of sleep. Sleep is fragile. We can't force it to happen. The harder we try, the further it retreats. Sleep entails letting go.

Like many others, I often awaken after a few hours then have trouble falling back to sleep. My mind quickly turns to issues from the day before and fears about the day ahead. I am still embarrassed about that missed appointment. I dread the discussion with a difficult employee. The printer finally broke down; do I need a new one? What was that suspicious charge on my credit card? Why the snide remark?

Once in a while those deep-in-the-dark inner chats come up with a brilliant solution, but not very often. They usually leave me exhausted in the morning with little to show for the effort.

To fall asleep after waking during the night, we must release our thoughts and allow space to fill the field of awareness. I find it helpful to borrow from the practice of mindfulness meditation. Attend to the breathing, counting the breaths. Inhale. Exhale. Envision a candle, get lost in the flame. Imagine a favorite place. Repeat a soothing phrase. Try white noise (a fan or a sound machine) to focus attention without inciting thought.

The ability to influence our own thinking is a helpful skill. That skill can steer a negative train of thought onto a positive track. It can allow us to manage physical pain and to work our way through emotional distress. It can also contribute to physical energy by opening the door to restful and restoring sleep.

Is sleep a challenge for you? What about the body's other basic needs? What one thing could you do to energize the body and its impact on other dimensions of your life?

Fight, Flee, Embrace

Emotional energy governs the movement of the heart toward and away from other human beings. It checks out the stranger and determines in an instant whether she is friend or foe. Approach, engage. Avoid, retreat. Fight, flee, or embrace.

All dimensions of energy are influenced by our thoughts. We noted earlier that even the restful sleep required for physical energy pivots on events in the mind. Emotional energy is likewise enhanced when we carefully monitor, direct and express our thinking about others.

Blame, anger, judgment, and the struggle for control arise from thoughts that sap the flow of energy and stop the power of engagement in its tracks. Acceptance, gratitude, forgiveness, and cooperation are expressed in thoughts that free the heart to join another in work and play on the ground of our common humanity.

I recently witnessed a group of women in the locker room griping about household appliances. As I hurried to dress, my happy post-workout mood weakened with tales of faulty refrigerators and microwave ovens. It was such a relief to walk outside and celebrate the day by re-calibrating the contents of my mind.

If a rant about stoves and garbage disposals can be so disruptive, how much more does our energy suffer from harsh thoughts about other people? Whether we dwell on distant political and military conflicts or on the annoying habits of our nearest and dearest, a catalog of grievances is not the fuel for a positive flame.

Setting aside the critical thought, diverting the destructive conversation, and replacing judgment with benefit-of-the-doubt takes awareness and commitment. The rewards in emotional energy are worth the effort. With the full engagement of emotional energy, we can embrace one other and enjoy the differences that add up to whole much better than its parts.

Think for a moment about one of your most challenging "others." What can you find to appreciate? How might you reach out, connect, and heal?

Bang! Bang! Pause

Bang! Pause. Bang Bang!! Pause. Pause. B-b-b-b-bang! We love our fireworks. New Year's Eve in Missoula doesn't outdo the Fourth of July, but it tries hard.

I love the New Year and its message of a fresh start. I take energy from putting away the past year of experience along with the Christmas decorations. Highlights have been shared in our holiday letter. Low points have been harvested for lessons learned and set aside. Then, bang! The starter's gun fires, and we are off. Resolutions and to-do lists in hand, we surge forward with high energy and ambitious plans. Or not. What about the pause?

One recent New Year I re-committed to meditation. As a high school student, I loved visiting the monastery, kneeling in silence while votive candles flickered on a side altar and monks chanted the Hours. I have dabbled in reflective practice ever since, and in retirement have relished the luxury of starting the day slowly. Still, meditation calls for specific commitment. It is so easy to fall out of the habit. I am tempted to start the day instead with the energy of strong coffee and an action plan. Why not start with a bang?

Over the years, I have found that action disembodied from purpose falls short. I go out strong, but before long I collapse in frustration. On the other hand, I am fulfilled when efforts are grounded in meaning. I gain energy when pieces fit into place and create a greater whole. When I start the day with meditative listening, it leads toward peaceful productivity: centered and balanced and guided by a sense of direction.

Athletes know that it is critical to warm up before a race. Muscles and tendons, heart and lungs must be awake and tuned in before the starter fires the gun. My mind also needs to ease into the day. After reflection they are ready for coffee and action. Bang!

How do the best mornings begin for you? What would you change if you decided to try something new?

How Are You?

Hi, Happy New Year! Great to see you, it's been too long. How are you? Busy. Me too. Let's get together sometime. Yes, let's. I should have more time after I finish this class. Hi, how are you? Busy. We're remodeling. Hi, how are you? Busy. Company coming. Hi, how are you? Too busy. Work is a zoo. Sigh.

We have a cultural bias toward busyness. If I am busy, I am important and my life matters. If I am busy, I can claim my place at the table with the producers. If I am busy, my life work is fulfilling and I feel good about myself.

But what about the other side of that view? When I am busy, I do not see the beauty in the moment. When I am busy, I resent your call and hurry to finish. When I am busy I don't find time to visit when you are suffering. When I am busy, I skip my workout and eat fast food from the drive-through. When I am busy, I am always off and running to the next thing.

Everyone has the same amount of time. The President. The toddler. The homeless. The incarcerated. The professional. The monk. The laborer. The dying. Those who are in love. Those who are waiting for important news. Why, then do we see the passage of time in such different terms? For some, time is about waiting; for others, filling it up. For some, too much; for others, not enough.

Our experience of time is a function of both our circumstances and our perceptions. Busyness is as much a state of our mind as it is the snapshot of our calendar. We recently reflected on meditation, on taking a moment to pause before launching the day. Now I am exploring the image of life as meditation, aware of what is happening now and responding in the moment.

The quality of my presence and the value of my response are grounded in space. White space on the calendar, clear space in the mind, open space in the heart. Busyness fills those spaces. The busy me is not always the best me. I am more available when "Busy" is not the answer to "How are you?" I am a better listener when my mind does not race to the next meeting or task. I am healthier when I take time to cook, even if it means saying "no" to an enticing project. The quality of my effort suffers when quantity comes first.

How do you balance busyness with presence, productivity with reflection, quantity with quality?

Hoarding and Sorting

Though the meeting lasted less than an hour, it generated a hefty to-do list that was not there when it started. The same thing happened yesterday, and I suspect it will repeat tomorrow. That experience, in turn, led to my seeing the pattern as a variation on hoarding. I find common threads between an overcrowded basement and an overcrowded calendar. They both involve collecting and clinging: to stuff on the one hand, opportunities on the other.

I often express the reflexive "yes," especially since retiring from a regular job. I want to make good use of newly available time. I want to support the people I love and causes in which I believe. I am pretty good at resisting options that neither spark my passion nor align with my skills. My downfall comes with the abundance of opportunities that meet both criteria.

This morning, I am sitting at the coffee shop designing a new filter with a tighter grid. I want to develop a more effective process for determining which opportunities will become commitments. This new filter requires a project to have intrinsic value and personal reward; it must also fit realistically with other priorities into the bigger picture of the time ahead. When the collection overflows, I can replace lower priorities with higher ones. I can keep them all but change my degree of involvement. I can ask for help or I create a bucket list to revisit later.

It is time for spring cleaning. My closets and drawers are cluttered with things I no longer want or need. My to-do list is cluttered with responsibilities I have allowed to pile up unsorted. Space, time, and energy are overflowing. It is time to evaluate, to apply thoughtful priorities, and to take the steps needed to simplify my life.

What about your list? What about your calendar? What about your energy budget? Is it time for a change?

Let There Be Light

For about a week, I have felt the batteries running down. My mind is as sharp and clear as cotton wool. Motivation hovers, with the overnight lows, below zero. The open calendar that is normally a source of energy and delight stares back at me vacantly, asking "So now that you have free time, what are you going to do with it?"

It is the day after solstice, and I am wondering how much this pattern has to do with sun. It is the weekend before Christmas, and "holiday blues" might play a part. Lyle is helping his family far away, and a degree of loneliness factors into the mix. As I reflect on the lassitude, I feel some momentum creeping back in. It is helpful to face the experience and name it, not just to curl up and escape. It is also helpful to notice the lengthening days. Yesterday was the day of longest night. It has come and gone. Now I want to turn around, face the sunrise, and look forward to the cycle of renewal that lies ahead.

Although I love the coziness of winter and the warm glow of a fire and Christmas tree in predawn darkness, I celebrate the sun's return. Though imperceptible at first, this day next week will be three minutes longer than today. In a month it will gain thirty-nine minutes, and in three months nearly four hours to celebrate the equinox.

The sun is an important source of mental and emotional energy, and the shift from shrinking to growing days is bound to help my outlook. I also look forward to shifting my focus past the holidays as a centerpiece. Holiday blues for me come with any contrast between seasonal ideals and current reality. This year, we made the difficult decision to spend Christmas Day apart for the first time in 35 years. It was a complex decision rooted in family values, but it did leave frayed loose ends to be mended in the New Year.

White space on the calendar is most valuable when scarce, and ironically it has grown for me this year as Christmas nears. Holiday letters and gifts were mailed early. Parties, holiday concerts, and TV specials peaked, then waned. My calendar is open while others fill their time with shopping, cleaning, and cooking for the big day.

My energy is low. The energy of the sun and the energy of a busy life are low. With midwinter, the turning point is here. Tomorrow will have more daylight than today. Next week the holidays will pass and everyday tasks and social contacts will return. In the meantime, I will rest and feed the spirit and trust that my own energy will be recharged as well.

What are your sources of energy? How do you handle the natural ebb and flow that results when they change?

People Power

Many of us celebrated when Susan Cain's thoughtful treatise, *Quiet,* made the bestseller list a few years back. For the first time, the real challenges and gifts of people with an introverted temperament came into everyday conversation. At last, someone understood us and we didn't feel quite so weird.

Introverts do not dislike people. They are not necessarily awkward in social settings. They do need time alone to recharge. We go to the party and may have fun, but the next day finds us curled up with a book. If our work involves teamwork, Friday nights are for jammies and old movies at home. I am an introvert. I am always looking for the white spaces sprinkled through an active life.

Sometimes, however, the balance tips and I go too far: I get ahead with chores, catch up on errands, and decline new commitments. At such times, I face not only a single welcome day of solitude, but a longer stretch of time on my own. Those occasions help me see life from another perspective. I begin feeling the urge to connect, to be in a crowd, and to have some noise (almost any noise) breaking up the silence. It happened again last week.

It would have been easy to call a friend for coffee or to join a group for a run; but by the time I noticed, my batteries were too low. As I discovered with our car several months back, a battery can discharge past the point of "jumping." Like starting a car, social initiative takes energy and I was out of it. Fortunately, time and friends were prepared to heal; after a few blank days, a generous array of holiday invitations appeared on the calendar.

While watching my energy ebb and flow, I realized the importance of people power in a quiet life. When others share their joy with me, I respond in kind. The exchange of thoughts and feelings, laughter and fun get the juices flowing again. Yes, I may be an introvert, but not all the time. As with my car, I have learned a lesson about personal batteries. Next time I will remember to pull out the jumper cables and connect with others before it is too late.

How do you balance the energy of together and alone? How have you recharged by tapping into the energy of others who are willing to share?

Seasons

To be interested in the changing seasons is a happier frame of mind than to be hopelessly in love with spring.
George Santayana

When we talk about the reasons we like to live one place or another, many of us cite the cycle of distinct seasons as a plus. While it is fun to go south in winter or north in summer, to the tropics or the arctic for a change in pace, we appreciate the fact that each season has its gift. Each season also has its drawbacks. I take energy from the cycles and changes, and observe repeating patterns that come with equinox and solstice again and again and again.

Winter Driving

Earlier that week, we cut our holiday cabin-stay a day short. It was not an easy decision, but ominous weather made a compelling case. A large green blob of moisture on the weather maps approached from the Pacific Coast. A surge of white and negative numbers descended from the Arctic. They converged on the highway toward home on the day we had planned to leave.

In weighing the implications, my view of a successful trip sharpened significantly. I wanted two things, and I wanted them very much: visibility and traction. The forecast of ground fog, blowing snow, and black ice was unsettling. We headed home. As we drove, I reflected on the importance of traction and visibility in life's larger journey. "Where am I? How will I get there?" Those are good questions for the New Year.

Visibility while driving allows us to see what's coming and to adjust. We can see the sign pointing to our turn-off, move around a slow truck on the steep grade, and avoid elk crossing the road. Visibility in life enables us to keep our goals in view, working our way through challenges and around obstacles that may arise.

Traction while driving gives us solid contact with the road. It enables us to accelerate confidently, to negotiate curves, and to brake smoothly to a stop when needed. Traction in our lives gives us solid contact with our deepest values. It stabilizes our journey, holding us to the path while we navigate the adventures, the growth, and the setbacks of everyday life.

In preparing a fresh New Year's beginning for this segment of life's journey, I have been thinking in terms of winter driving. Where am I going? What do I want to achieve in the year ahead? Is the vision clear enough that I can follow signs to the proper exit? Will I be able to see the potholes, the curves, the "bridge out" warnings up ahead? How am I tracking? Am I solidly grounded in values as I move forward?

What is your vision of success in the coming year? Is it clear and compelling enough to guide your way? How will you maintain traction and avoid sliding off the course?

Shades of Gray

Wrapped in a fuzzy blanket on the recliner and looking out over the valley, I napped after breakfast for more than an hour. My mind was quiet. Emotions soft and receptive. Senses at rest. Energy low.

I was tempted to call it depression, but asked for the wisdom of a different name. What if we saw the condition called "SAD" not as a disorder but as an evolutionary gift? What would it look and feel like if I gave thanks instead of searching for a cure? The shades of gray clouds and brown grass with patches of melting snow are subdued. They turn me inward. They trigger a desire to hibernate and wait for the sun to reappear. Maybe that is a good thing.

Our cultural standard and my personal expectation are for incessant high and productive energy. When that expectation is unfulfilled, something seems wrong. I put on lively music, shop for a special lamp, and infuse my system with caffeine to counter the mood.

Our primitive ancestors did not have special lamps, iPods, or espresso. In winter they were challenged to survive the cold and bridge a season of scarcity. Over thousands of years, those who hunkered down on a gray day conserved resources and emerged intact with the spring. Those who defied conditions and insisted on an active winter may have run out of juice before the sun returned.

No, I am not giving in and giving up on the active life. I live in a heated home, have abundant food, and enjoy a closet full of warm clothing that allows me to thrive outdoors. On the other hand, I am listening with more compassion to ancestral voices. Perhaps some days are made for recovery, for snoozing, for letting go and letting be. I don't always need to fight back and fix them but can accept and receive, appreciate and learn. Today feels like one of those days.

The palette of life offers a full range of tones: from red to blue and white to black, with shades of gray and brown. Each color has its place in the larger picture. I pray for the wisdom to appreciate them all.

How do you experience the quieter and darker tones of winter? Friend, foe, or some of each?

April Showers

I am so ready to welcome April…yes, even its showers! March in my life this year was a test from beginning to end. I don't know (or really care, right now) whether I passed the test. I am ready to turn over the calendar and start a new month.

One morning this week I woke up to the familiar sight of clouds in the valley. I sighed, tallied one more gray day on the mental calendar, and went on with business. Later, however, I had a chance to drive out into the country. When I got out of the car, I smelled spring! I smelled fresh, damp earth. When I looked harder, the sheet of ice sealing the ground was breaking up. I could almost envision a green tinge to the tan hillside. I felt a surge of inner joy.

For the first time this year, I really believed in spring. At a visceral level, I responded to the change of seasons. The date on the calendar didn't do it. Daylight Savings Time didn't do it. It took the reflexive response of bodily senses to convince me: It is time to start anew.

New Year's Day. First Day of School. And more. There are many dates and seasons, each with its own rituals, that trigger list-making, fresh starts, and resolutions for a better life. I have not typically viewed spring as one of those times. My friend Frank, who is a gardener, knows how to celebrate the season. Buy seeds. Plant. April showers bring May flowers. Those of us with purple thumbs may see it as the wet brown season between lovely white and iridescent green.

I am a convert! Not to gardening necessarily, but to spring. I am ready for the rain. I am ready for the mud. I am ready for the lighter clothing. I am ready to phase out of skis and ease into hiking boots. Goodbye treadmill, hello trail. It has been a long and beautiful winter. Time for something else. Spring does not mean marking time between the "better" seasons, but has a charm worthy of celebrating in its own right. One of those charms in Montana is that tomorrow might be winter again. To be embraced in its own right.

What does this season mean for you? What rituals do you look forward to? Gardening? A spring break trip to warmer weather? Spring skiing until every last patch of white is gone?

Dust Bunnies

Because the days of spring are getting longer, even the inevitable snow showers and cold snaps are releasing their hold on the landscape. We are carried by the irresistible force of nature towards green hills, birds, and flowers. We want to get outside and play. That's what spring is all about!

Well, maybe not "all" that it's about. Most of us grew up with yet another seasonal tradition: spring cleaning. For my mother, spring meant scrubbing the house from stem to stern. Furniture was moved, dust bunnies hunted down and exterminated. Windows were washed, and floors, and walls. Smooth cotton linens replaced fuzzy flannel ones.

My own version of the ritual is somewhat less dramatic and much less thorough. I do enjoy dusting and vacuuming, opening windows and wiping off grime. I love the practice of swapping clothes from one part of the closet to another, and I take satisfaction from purging the collected clutter and heading for the thrift shop.

This year, I have also been thinking of spring cleaning with a broader view as I scrutinize my calendar, budget, and to-do list. I have been evaluating the contents of my email inbox and Facebook news feed. I have been observing my daily habits with a critical eye. What am I doing "just because?" Where am I ready to move on? How do I want to invest the new energy that comes with more sun and fewer clothes?

The box for the thrift shop went out yesterday. I hope the bargains inside add enjoyment to someone else's life. The calendar, the budget, the in-box, and the to-do list are slimming down and changing too. I am making room in my life as well as in my closet. Room in my mind as well as my house. Room to welcome the next unexpected gift from the Universe with an open heart, rather than groaning inside and wondering "What will I do with THAT?"

How is excess baggage unbalancing your load? What would you like to pass along to someone who would enjoy it more?

Alaskan Summer

I woke up this morning to a gray sky with wisps of cloud and fog outlining the creases between mountains. Summer is short in the northern Rockies, and we who live here get crabby on cloudy days in June. A few years ago, I was surprised to find that I could transform the landscape and its impact with a slight shift in perspective.

The mystique of Alaska has enveloped my adult imagination. The fantasy of living there has passed, but photographs and memories from three wonderful trips have enhanced my inner vision with dramatic landscapes. If I look out on Missoula in June from just the right angle, I see the Alaska of my dreams and crabbiness goes away. This annual experience reinforces the truth that we create the world we see. The brain draws from its file folders of life experience to interpret the sights, sounds, smells, tastes, and touches that flood our everyday lives.

In some cases the senses trigger delight: the aroma of warm chocolate chip cookies, the silken texture of cat fur, or the gurgle of a stream trickling through rocks. Other impressions signal alarm: flashing red lights in the rear-view mirror, a bear on the trail, the doctor's message that something looks suspicious. From one extreme to another, we continually filter incoming data through past experience and its emotional tone.

Until recently, those mental filters have been seen as intractable personal traits that resist change. However, brain research teaches us that ineffective thought patterns can intentionally be discarded and new ones designed. Overlaying a cloudy Montana day with the Alaskan mystique improves my outlook. Understanding my friend more deeply converts irritation into compassion. Re-working dismay over a near-miss gives way to gratitude for the disaster that almost-but-didn't-quite materialize and for lessons learned to use the next time.

What is your experience of changing mental channels to find one that works better or that improves your emotional response?

Longest Day

It is the summer solstice. Sunlight reigns dominant this one day before gradually yielding to darkness. A friend tells me that she is always sad on the longest day. As a sun lover, she feels the turning point with pain. I have never seen it that way. For me, today is the beginning of summer. Snow is melting off the passes, flowers are blooming, rivers and spirits are running high. My mood is on the upswing.

Over the past week, I could appreciate my friend's perspective from a different angle, as I was tested for two unrelated health issues. Neither of the results is reassuring. Both point to a future that could change the way I enjoy life. Neither of the results is urgent; both are cautionary. Nothing changed the way I feel physically. The change is in my mind and heart.

Those test results are a type of turning point, like the summer solstice. They point to unwelcome changes and signify aging and mortality. They call for attention and adjustment. They do not, however, mean I must forsake the healthy joy I have today. I can choose to prematurely grieve a future loss or to live fully with gratitude for every moment on its own terms. I am still working on it!

How do the dynamics of present and future play out for you? Do you fret over what might happen, or do you celebrate the present and let the future unfold when and as it will?

Dry Lightning

Western Montana is the stuff of legend. Big skies. Big timber. Big game. Big rivers. Those of us who live here would consider nowhere else. Until it happens again: Big fires. Big smoke.

Since the millennium, fire season has grown. It starts earlier, lasts longer, and burns more brightly in between. This change (is it climate?) is West-wide and growing. Montana is not, for all its other charms, immune. The time comes most years when we can no longer see across the valley. We might no longer see across the street. Breathing is an issue. Activity is discouraged. Life grinds to a miserable halt or proceeds against advice despite it all.

At the checkout line, everyone is talking: another evacuation. Slurry bombers ferry retardant from the airport through the smoke and grumble into the distance. Helicopters lift buckets of water from the river and drop protection on wildland homes. Smokejumpers strap on parachutes and head off to the front lines.

Yes, we are living the dream. But homeowners in exile are praying for the wind to shift. We can't see; our eyes burn. We can't breathe; our chests are tight. And we look for rain that doesn't come. The dream is hidden behind the smoke. For how long?

I struggle to remember the choices I have when facing reality: Resist, escape, or accept. Accepting reality is the only peaceful option, yet it's so very hard.

What aspect of reality comes unbidden and overstays its welcome for you? How do you deal with the inevitable days when it's all outside your control?

Cooler, Darker, Busier

According to the paper, bears are eating twenty hours a day, storing up fat to last through winter. Seated comfortably at the kitchen table, I find myself following suit. There is a powerful urge to eat more carbs, eat more fats, and fill to overflowing. The paper also notes that sun arrives today at 7:30 a.m. and departs at 7:30 p.m. Maybe that is why I find it so hard to wake up early for reflection or exercise and why I lurch into the day groggy and unfocused.

Autumn is a spectacular season and a favorite for many of us. Clear days with a crisp nip around the edges generate energy. Turning colors are brilliant against deep blue skies. The harvest is ripe and farmers' markets abound with colors and tastes to savor and put away for later. Autumn is also, however, a time of transition, and transitions call for re-calibrating our expectations.

The seasons provide a convenient framework for reflection and anticipation. With the solstice and the equinox, we have a chance to look back, learn from, and celebrate the season that is coming to a close. We can also look ahead to what in our lives is changing, and adjust where needed. Students, teachers, and parents struggle to meet the demands of school and sports. Hunters scout the territory and sort their gear. Football fans gather around tailgates. Plants set seed and birds migrate.

Transitions are times of disruption and times of growth. We can hold our breath and wait for them to pass or we can light the spirit to enjoy the adventure. Make the choice, and energy will follow.

How do you maintain healthy habits when the seasons change? How does the onset of fall trigger new approaches to exercise, eating, rest, and relationships?

Tipping the Balance

It is 7:00 a.m., and the slightest hint of gray anticipates dawn. Somewhere in the recesses of slumber and darkness I missed the intention to rise earlier. Last week the balance tipped in the northern hemisphere. It tipped toward darkness and away from light. Little voices in my head argued for a few more minutes in bed before we launched the day. I will be setting an alarm for the next few weeks, until I get used to the change.

As a "transition junkie" I find it invigorating to pack away one set of clothes and hang up another, shift in the mornings from a sunrise view to the cozy fireside chair, dust off the treadmill, and re-pack my gym bag.

Autumn offers its gifts in the beauty of changing leaves and the vitality of frosty mornings. It brings us back to school—whether in fact or in spirit—as crossing guards, fall sports, and students with laptops appear. It is a time for canning and freezing to preserve the harvest. Hunting to fill the freezer. Cutting, splitting, and stacking wood to feed the fire.

Autumn also issues unique challenges as we resume a framework of structure and responsibility. Business meetings resume. Phones ring. Calendars fill. Classes convene. Homework fills the gaps. We may miss the dominance of day and go reluctantly into night.

A change of seasons calls us to re-balance our lives. Just as the equinox—that one day of perfect symmetry between daylight and darkness—passes quickly, the balance in our lives is always in flux. I wonder whether the season is called "fall" because that's what happens when we don't adjust in time?

What are the gifts of autumn for you? What are the challenges? How will you adapt to seasonal changes this time around?

Fall Back, Play it Again

As a coach, I work with people who want to live more effective lives. In the process, I am impressed with the role of reflection in personal growth. This weekend, as we turn back the clocks in adjusting to winter's darker days, I am inclined to use that ritual as a reminder to reflect. This one day of the year, we have a chance to re-live the hour in a miniature time warp. We are drinking our morning coffee. The clock says seven. Voila! The clock says six. How do we want to spend that extra hour, using the insights we gained from living it the first time?

Reflection is the act of stepping back from direct experience and viewing it from a distance. With a different perspective, we can see ourselves from the outside and observe our thoughts, feelings, and choices as if they belonged to someone else. We can ask ourselves questions that allow us to probe more deeply, understand more clearly, and learn from experience. We can chart a new course that enables us to try new approaches to opportunity and challenge.

As we charge toward winter, I find myself reflecting on lessons I have learned year after year with seasonal change. I recall the familiar urge to hunker down, eat more, and conserve energy. I have trouble getting up, out, and about. Reflection reminds me that healthy eating and exercise now can get me through this tight spot and into a happy new year. I have learned that active is better than passive in navigating the transition from fall into the winter holiday season.

How do you maintain a commitment to wellness through seasonal change? Given the chance to play it again, what will you do to take a cue from past successes and setbacks?

Grateful Anyway

As the holiday season nears, I have an instinctive urge to reflect on Thanksgiving. Still, what can be thought or said that has not become trite with overuse? Gratitude is "in." We have gratitude journals and gratitude calendars. It is a healthy trend, and I am pleased to join the crowd. Nevertheless, the tendency to give thanks can skim the surface or it can plunge the depths. Let's look just an inch or two below the obvious and see what we find.

Family, friends, and health. These are the things we commonly mention when asked to give thanks. A job, a home, enough food. The first thoughts that come to mind would, if we completed the sentence, end, "I give thanks because so many people don't have what I am taking for granted."

What would it mean for us to give thanks when our health has taken a hit, family members are fighting, and friends fall short? Is it possible to be grateful when jobless, homeless, and hungry? My own exposure to loss and deprivation is limited. I have, however, learned from others that giving thanks is a human privilege whatever the condition of our lives. In fact, the most powerful message comes from gratitude that emerges from setbacks, frustrations, and painful realities.

Without the divorce, his door would not have opened to a new life with a different partner, children, and extended family. Being fired taught her to clarify her strengths, confront her shortcomings, and turn her life around. Cancer focused all of their energy on appreciating, affirming, and fighting for life without sweating the small stuff. A financial crisis brought lessons about the generosity of others and the value of a simpler life. Clouds have silver linings, though they are rarely evident at first.

I have been experimenting with a new practice around this belief. When something goes wrong and I hear myself begin to say "I am so angry (or frustrated, or bored)," I try to substitute "grateful" for the negative word. That usually makes me laugh. Who am I kidding? But then I go on and finish the sentence with "because…." In taking that step, I actively look for a silver lining, and it's always there. For example, one recently transformed sentence read, "I am so grateful for the speeding ticket because it reminds me to slow down in a school zone and watch for children in the street."

Where in your life is thanks-giving hard to come up with? Dig deeper. What is your version of a silver lining? I believe it is there.

Solstice

The warm red darkness centers on a flickering fire. Christmas lights on the mantel cast a gentle aura on the wall. Candlelight bobs and dances. My soul savors the timelessness of sitting and watching, surrounded by softly playing carols on the radio.

Back in September, when we observed the equinox, I was a little sad. Daylight was losing the competition, and darkness was asserting its dominance for another six months. I forget from year to year how much I love midwinter. I love getting up before the sun, before the neighbors, long before my husband the night person. I love the quiet. I love the beauty of lights when darkness prevails and the power of song when vision is muted.

The call to action is less compelling in the dark. I am content to be, not just to do. I sense the connection of my life with Life itself. I let go of thought and embrace intuition. I feel the heartbeats settle and the breathing even out.

The Christmas story fits so well into its midwinter setting. Cold, darkness, holiday travel, crowded lodgings, and paying taxes set the stage. A kind innkeeper and patient livestock offer refuge to a young pregnant woman and her husband. Angels and shepherds and wise men complete the picture. Almost.

Before dawn in Bethlehem, a baby is born. His message will change the world for those who hear with an open heart. Before dawn in Missoula, I listen for the whisper of messages. They are easier to discern in the deep quiet of midwinter darkness, when life's other demands are hidden by the shadows.

It is the winter solstice. I celebrate its place in the cycle of my inner year. I am tempted to feel a little sad as daylight asserts itself and starts its trek toward dominance. But then I remember, "to everything there is a season and a time for every purpose under heaven."

What are the gifts of midwinter for you? What do you savor? How do you celebrate?

Afterword

A friend who reviewed the draft of *Going Deeper* asked whether I intended to end in midwinter darkness with a reflection on the Solstice. That was a great question, and I gave it some thought. It wasn't an accidental ending, nor had I made the decision with clear awareness and full intent. For some reason it felt right at the time.

Now, months later, it still feels right. My reflective writing most often takes shape early in the morning, while my mind is still quiet and imagination receptive. Here in Montana, those early mornings are most often dark. The winter solstice captures the setting in which these words have been born. Yes, I guess I did intend to end there, and further reflection strengthens that intent.

The silent darkness of early morning is a creative time. It is a time for plunging the deeper dimensions of life and for bringing them forward into the light of wisdom and transformation.

Resources

Books

Cain, Susan. *Quiet: The Power of Introverts in a World that Can't Stop Talking*
Casey, Karen. *Daily Meditations for Practicing the Course*
Catalano, Tim; Goucher, Adam; Mills, Billy. *Running the Edge*
Combs, Deidre. *Worst Enemy, Best Teacher*
Csikszentmihalyi, Mihaly. *Flow*
Drucker, Peter. *Management: Tasks, Responsibilities, Practices*
Graham, Linda. *Bouncing Back*
Galloway, Jeff. *Running Until You're 100*
Hanson, Rick and Mendius, Richard. *Buddha's Brain*
Hobday, José. *Simple Living*
Hobday, José. *Stories of Awe and Abundance*
Jampolsky, Gerald. *Love Is Letting Go of Fear*
Huston, Paula. *Simplifying the Soul*
Karr, Alphonse. *Sur la Plage (On the Beach)*
Keller, Helen. *The Open Door*
Loehr, Jim and Schwartz, Tony. *The Power of Full Engagement*
Merton, Thomas. *No Man Is an Island*
Newton, Sir Isaac. *Philosphiae Naturalis Principia Mathematica*
Padmasambhava. *Tibetan Book of the Dead*
Palmer, Parker. *Let Your Life Speak*
Rosen, Mark I. *Thank You for Being Such a Pain*
Seligman, Martin. *Learned Optimism*
Silverstein, Shel. *The Giving Tree*
Tolle, Eckhart. *The Power of Now*

Other Media

Bendjellou, Malik. *Searching for Sugar Man* (documentary film)
Brickman, Marshall and Elice, Rick. *Jersey Boys* (play)
Hammerstein, Oscar. *The Sound of Music* (musical)
Henderson, Sarah; Hollister, Geoff; Lyttle, Erich. *There Is No Finish Line: The Joan Benoit Samuelson Story* (documentary film)
Hanson, Rick. *Just One Thing* (e-newsletter)
Lennon, John. *Beautiful Boy* (song)
Massey, Morris. *What You Are is Where You Were When* (videotaped lecture)
Saucony. *Find Your Strong Project*, www.saucony.com (webpage)
Seeger, Pete. *Turn Turn Turn* (song)
Zapiks. *Speed Riding-Antoine Montant-Can't Stop* www.zapiks.com/speed-riding-antoine-montant-1.html (video)

Note: The resources listed above are referenced in *Going Deeper*. Some quotations used in the book are taken from websites that quote an individual but do not specify a source document. Those quotations are not listed here, but are attributed to their authors where cited in the text. If a source document for the quotation is also identified, that document is listed here.

Acknowledgments

Jane Darnell and I met at a business meeting. We compared our experiences as slow but impassioned distance runners. After we had returned from that meeting to our separate hometowns, we began emailing about our marathon training. The horizon broadened to a full range of topics as we gained trust and treasured the interaction. After I retired from the Forest Service and embarked on a life-coaching practice, Jane encouraged me to expand the dialogue we had shared by writing for a larger audience. I am grateful to Jane for everything she has given me. She has been there from the beginning and remains a reliable source of support for my adventure in writing.

When I began to publish weekly *Reflections*, I invited some like-minded friends to join my mailing list. With a heartening response to fuel the effort, our shared journey took off at a brisk pace. I cast my fellow travelers as "wellbuddies" on the path to improving health and happiness. Over the years, I have posted *Reflections* every Sunday morning. Each week, different readers have responded from their own experience and perspective, engaging actively in the reflective endeavor. I am grateful to my wellbuddies for encouraging me to reflect, to write, and to share; and for enriching my experience with their own.

After four years of weekly *Reflections*, a number of readers asked me to consider a book. They wanted to revisit their favorite essays collected under a single cover. I was daunted by the prospect, as I had so much to learn. Knowing I needed a team approach, I asked the readership for help. A diverse cross-section of fans and friends stepped forward.

During a year (or so) of traveling the road to publication, I have engaged my cadre of "book buddies" by tossing out ideas, asking for feedback, and reporting on progress. In return, I have received invaluable advice and the encouragement to keep moving, especially when I felt stuck. I want to thank the following for sharing their wisdom and expertise in playing the book-buddy role: Cheryl Bela, Jane Darnell, Kimberly Dredger, Gwen Florio, Sharon Friedman, Karla Hawley, Claire Huking, Marge Hulburt, Sherry Munther, Bunny Sims, Lucia Solorzano, and Sue Vap.

Author

Pam Gardiner grew up in Indiana and Ohio at the beginning of the Baby Boom. She decided early on that she wanted to help others with their personal development. College majors in philosophy and psychology followed by a master's degree in counseling got her started on that path.

After a few years of work with high school and college students, however, she had second thoughts about her initial career choice. A second cycle of undergraduate study in botany was aimed in the direction of an academic career that also stopped short of its intended goal.

Serendipitous events led instead to an unexpected career with the United States Forest Service. Beginning as a front desk receptionist, Gardiner grew professionally over the years into filling a series of leadership roles. Two years before retirement, she was invited to serve as a learning coach for the agency's senior leadership training program. That experience rekindled her early passion for helping others develop, both professionally and personally.

After she retired, Gardiner trained with and was certified by Wellcoaches School of Coaching. While developing a coaching practice, Gardiner started to write *Reflections*, a weekly email exploring personal growth topics. *Going Deeper* draws 100 favorite *Reflections* from more than 250 written during its first five years.

Gardiner also volunteers for her local running club. She coaches a marathon training program and founded the Back of the Pack, a program for slower runners and walkers in the club.

Pam Gardiner and her husband, Lyle Geurts, live in Missoula, Montana. Their son and his wife, Jonathan and Jennie Geurts, live in Colorado.

Made in the USA
Charleston, SC
16 October 2014